Rigor in Your Classroom

Teachers are required to increase the rigor for students, but how? This book by bestselling author and rigor expert Barbara Blackburn has the answer! It is a treasure chest of more than 200 practical and highly effective tools that can be used across grade levels and subject areas to increase student rigor, leading your students to higher engagement and deeper learning.

Topics covered include . . .

- ♦ Asking higher-level questions

- ♦ Scaffolding to help all students achieve success

- ♦ Differentiating instruction and using modifications

- ♦ Fostering independence through gradual release of responsibility

- ♦ Increasing text difficulty and teaching close reading

- ♦ Setting high expectations

- ♦ Changing students' views of success

- ♦ Encouraging effort and goal-setting

- ♦ Creating an environment that is conducive to learning

- ♦ Using effective grading policies and assessment tools

- ♦ Working with parents, colleagues, and administrators

- ♦ And much, much more!

Rigor in Your Classroom will be your go-to resource throughout the school year, as you continually return to it to try new tools with your students. Bonus: The tools are accompanied by graphic organizers, charts, templates, and reproducibles for easy implementation.

Dr. Barbara R. Blackburn is the bestselling author of fourteen books and is a sought-after consultant. She was an award-winning professor at Winthrop University and has taught early childhood, elementary, middle, and high school students.

Also Available from Barbara R. Blackburn

(www.routledge.com/eyeoneducation)

Rigor Is Not a Four-Letter Word, Second Edition

Rigor for Students with Special Needs (with Bradley Witzel)

Rigor Made Easy: Getting Started

Rigor in Your School: A Toolkit for Leaders (with Ronald Williamson)

Rigorous Schools and Classrooms: Leading the Way (with Ronald Williamson)

Classroom Motivation from A to Z: How to Engage Your Students in Learning

Classroom Instruction from A to Z: How to Promote Student Learning

Literacy from A to Z: Engaging Students in Reading, Writing, Speaking, and Listening

Rigor in Your Classroom

A Toolkit for Teachers

Barbara R. Blackburn

Routledge
Taylor & Francis Group

NEW YORK AND LONDON

First published 2014
by Routledge
711 Third Avenue, New York, NY 10017

and by Routledge
2 Park Square, Milton Park, Abingdon, Oxon OX14 4RN

Routledge is an imprint of the Taylor & Francis Group, an informa business

Library of Congress Cataloging-in-Publication Data

Blackburn, Barbara R., 1961–
    Rigor in your classroom : a toolkit for teachers / Barbara R. Blackburn.
        pages cm
    Includes bibliographical references.
    1. School improvement programs.   2. Academic achievement.   3. Teaching.
I. Title.
    LB2822.8.B528 2014
    371.2'07—dc23
    2013040894

ISBN: 978-0-415-73472-1 (hbk)
ISBN: 978-0-415-73287-1 (pbk)
ISBN: 978-1-315-81978-5 (ebk)

Typeset in Palatino LT Std
by Apex CoVantage, LLC

Printed and bound in the United States of America by Sheridan Books, Inc. (a Sheridan Group Company).

To my sister Brenda, who evidences high expectations
for herself and all those around her.

Contents

3 Raise Expectations Through Questioning and Adult Behaviors 37

7 Reinvigorate the Environment 161

8   Extend Your Reach 187

Free Downloads

Many of the tools displayed in this book can be downloaded, printed, and copied for classroom use. You can access these downloads by visiting the book product page on our website: http://www.routledge.com/books/details/9780415732871. Then click on the tab that says "Supplemental Downloads," and click on the files. They will begin downloading to your computer.

Acknowledgments

To my wonderful husband, Pete, thank you for your encouragement, support, and love as I continue to do what I love.

Thank you to my family—my son Hunter, my parents, and my sisters for your patience as I sometimes get a little too focused!

Abbigail, a special thank you. You are always there when I need you, and even when I don't.

My appreciation to Ron Williamson, for his ideas, thoughts, and materials for Chapter 8: Extending Your Reach, Brad Witzel for his perspective on students with learning disabilities, and to Dani Sullivan for her creative ideas when I was stuck.

To Lauren Davis, my editor, thank you for always knowing how to take what I believe and help me turn it into something to share.

To Ann Linson, Jessica Schmettan, and Marianna White—thanks for your suggestions, which helped me clarify and refine the content.

To Jayne Varney, thank you for a wonderful cover design.

To Sandra Stafford and Apex CoVantage, thanks for the great jobs you did in copyediting and page make-up.

A special thank you to Reanna Young for production coordination.

To my new publisher, Routledge, thank you for giving me a wider audience for my books.

Finally, to the teachers and leaders in my workshops and all those who read my books and use the ideas to impact students, thank you. You make a difference every day in the lives of your students.

Meet the Author

Dr. Barbara Blackburn has dedicated her life to raising the level of rigor and motivation for professional educators and students alike. What differentiates Barbara's fourteen books are her easily executable concrete examples based on decades of experience as a teacher, professor, and consultant. Barbara's dedication to education was inspired in her early years by her parents. Her father's doctorate and lifetime career as a professor taught her the importance of professional training. Her mother's career as school secretary shaped Barbara's appreciation of the effort all staff play in the education of every child.

Barbara has taught early childhood, elementary, middle, and high school students and has served as an educational consultant for three publishing companies. She holds a master's degree in School Administration and is certified as a school principal in North Carolina. She received her Ph.D. in Curriculum and Teaching from the University of North Carolina at Greensboro. In 2006, she received the award for Outstanding Junior Professor at Winthrop University. She recently left her position at the University of North Carolina at Charlotte to write and speak full-time.

In addition to speaking at state and national conferences, she also regularly presents workshops for teachers and administrators in elementary, middle, and high schools. Her workshops are lively and engaging and filled with practical information. Her most popular topics include:

- Rigor is NOT a Four Letter Word
- Rigorous Schools and Classrooms: Leading the Way
- Motivation + Engagement + Rigor = Student Success
- Rigor for Students with Special Needs
- Instructional Strategies that Motivate Students
- Content Literacy Strategies for the Young and the Restless
- Motivating Yourself and Others
- Engaging Instruction Leads to Higher Achievement
- High Expectations and Increased Support Lead to Success

Introduction

Rigor in Your Classroom: A Toolkit for Teachers is a compilation of strategies to increase rigor for you and your students. What you'll find in each chapter is a wealth of ideas, far too many to be used immediately. I've designed it as a true toolkit—something you can go back to again and again to pull new ideas when you need them.

This book is different from my previous books for teachers on rigor: *Rigor is NOT a Four-Letter Word*, *Rigor Made Easy*, and *Rigor for Students with Special Needs*. *Rigor Made Easy* provided a quick start guide to rigor. *Rigor is NOT a Four-Letter Word* was designed for an in-depth analysis of rigor, with samples of classroom activities. *Rigor for Students with Special Needs* addressed a widely requested issue—how to incorporate rigor for students with learning disabilities.

Rigor in Your Classroom, on the other hand, paints a broad picture. You'll have a brief introduction to rigor, but then you have a treasure chest of ideas, one right after another, that you can choose from to tailor rigorous instruction for your class. The activities are appropriate preK-12th grade, and can be used across all subject areas.

In addition, I discuss how you can extend your reach beyond your students, to parents, administrators, and other teachers who work with you. There is an outline for a parent presentation (suitable for a PTA meeting), and online you'll find the accompanying PowerPoint as a free download; see page xv. No matter your situation, you'll find strategies you can use.

If you are an administrator, I encourage you to review *Rigor in Your School: A Toolkit for Leaders*. It focuses on leadership strategies you can use to increase rigor throughout your school.

Finally, I think you'll find the ideas to be very practical. Some are ones I used in my classroom, others are from teachers I know, and some are from other authors. No matter the source, my framework for choosing them was that you could immediately use the strategy to make a difference in your class. Enjoy!

1
Understanding Rigor

Instructional rigor is a key component of effective instruction. Too often, we think that our instruction is rigorous, but oftentimes it is not. Our assumptions about rigor, as well as our practices, make a difference in what we expect from students. In this chapter, we'll explore the myths of rigor, turn our attention to what true instructional rigor is, then look at the structure of the book.

Myths About Rigor

Despite all the research, there are seven commonly held myths about rigor. Let's look at each.

> **Seven Myths**
> 1. Lots of homework is a sign of rigor.
> 2. Rigor means doing more.
> 3. Rigor is not for everyone.
> 4. Providing support means lessening rigor.
> 5. Resources equal rigor.
> 6. Standards alone take care of rigor.
> 7. Rigor is just one more thing to do.

Myth 1: Lots of Homework is a Sign of Rigor

For many people the best indicator of rigor is the amount of homework required of students. Some teachers pride themselves on the amount of homework expected of their students, and there are parents who judge teachers by homework quantity. Realistically, all homework is not equally useful. Some of it is just busywork, assigned by teachers because principals or parents expect it. For some students, doing more homework in terms of quantity leads to burnout. When that occurs, students are less likely to complete homework, and may be discouraged about any learning activity.

Myth 2: Rigor Means Doing More

"Doing more" often means doing more low-level activities, frequently repetitions of things already learned. Such narrow and rigid approaches to learning do not define a rigorous classroom. Students learn in many different ways. Just as instruction must vary to meet the individual needs of students, so must homework. Rigorous and challenging learning experiences will vary with the student. Their design will vary; as will their duration. Ultimately, it is the quality of the assignment that makes a difference in terms of rigor.

Myth 3: Rigor is Not for Everyone

Often, teachers think the only way to assure success for everyone is to lower standards and lessen rigor. This may mask a hidden belief that some students can't really learn at high levels. You may have heard of the Pygmalion Effect—students live up to or down to our expectations of them. Each student can complete rigorous work at high levels, whether they are advanced or a student with special needs. Does the end result look different for those two students? Yes, but I know from my own experience as a teacher of struggling students reading far below their grade level that any teacher can be rigorous, and any student can reach higher levels with the right support.

Myth 4: Providing Support Means Lessening Rigor

In America, we believe in rugged individualism. We are to pull ourselves up by our bootstraps and do things on our own. Working in teams or accepting help is often seen as a sign of weakness. Supporting students so that they can learn at high levels is central to the definition of rigor. As teachers design lessons moving students toward more challenging work, they must provide scaffolding to support them as they learn.

Myth 5: Resources Equal Rigor

Recently, I've heard a common refrain. "If we buy this program, or textbook, or technology, then we would be rigorous." The right resources can certainly help increase the rigor in your classroom. However, raising the level of rigor for your students is not dependent on the resources you have. Think about the resources you have now. How can you use them more effectively? Do you use a textbook that includes true-false tests? Often, they are not rigorous because students can guess the answer. However, add one step for more rigor. Ask students to rewrite all false answers into true statements, and it requires students to demonstrate true understanding. It's not the resources; it's how you use them that make a difference.

Myth 6: Standards Alone Take Care of Rigor

Standards alone, even if they are rigorous, do not guarantee rigor in the classroom. The Common Core State Standards are designed to increase the level of rigor in classrooms across the nation. However, they were not designed to address instruction. In fact, they provide a framework for what is to be taught and what students are expected to know. If implemented without high levels of questioning or applications, the standards themselves are weakened. Your instructional practices, or how you implement standards, are just as critical as the curriculum.

Myth 7: Rigor is Just One More Thing To Do

Rigor is not another thing to add to your plate. Instead, rigor is increasing the level of expectation of what you are already doing. For example, if you are teaching vocabulary, instead of asking students to write their own definition of the word, ask them to write a riddle. It's the same end result, but at higher levels of Bloom's Taxonomy.

Defining Rigor

Now that we have looked at what rigor is *not*, let's look at what rigor *is*. In *Rigor is Not a Four Letter Word*, I define rigor as: Creating an environment in which:

- ♦ Each student is expected to learn at high levels.

- ♦ Each student is supported so he or she can learn at high levels.

- ♦ Each student demonstrates learning at high levels.

Notice we are looking at the environment you create. The tri-fold approach to rigor is not limited to the curriculum students are expected to learn. It is more than a specific lesson or instructional strategy. It is deeper than what a student says or does in response to a lesson. True rigor is the result of weaving together all elements of schooling to raise students to higher levels of learning. Let's take a deeper look at the three aspects of the definition.

Expecting Students to Learn at High Levels

The first component of rigor is creating an environment in which each student is expected to learn at high levels. Having high expectations starts with the recognition that every student possesses the potential to succeed at his or her individual level.

Almost every teacher or leader I talk with says, "We have high expectations for our students." Sometimes that is evidenced by the behaviors in the school; other times, however, faculty actions don't match the words. There are concrete ways to implement and assess rigor in classrooms.

As you design lessons that incorporate more rigorous opportunities for learning, you will want to consider the questions that are embedded in the instruction. Higher-level questioning is an integral part of a rigorous classroom. Look for open-ended questions, ones that are at the higher levels of Bloom's Taxonomy (analysis, synthesis). You'll find more on questioning in Chapter Three.

It is also important to pay attention to how you respond to student questions. When we visit schools, it is not uncommon to see teachers who ask higher-level questions. But for whatever reason, I then see some of the same teachers accept low-level responses from students. In rigorous classrooms, teachers push students to respond at high levels. They ask extending questions. Extending questions are questions that encourage a student to explain their reasoning and think through ideas. When a student does not know the immediate answer but has sufficient background information to provide a response to the question, the teacher continues to probe and guide the student's thinking rather than moving on to the next student. Insist on thinking and problem solving.

Supporting Students to Learn at High Levels

High expectations are important, but the most rigorous schools assure that each student is supported so he or she can learn at high levels, which is the second part of our definition. It is essential that teachers design lessons that move students to more challenging work while simultaneously providing ongoing scaffolding to support students' learning as they move to those higher levels.

Providing additional scaffolding throughout lessons is one of the most important ways to support your students. Oftentimes students have the ability or knowledge to accomplish a task, but are overwhelmed at the complexity of it, therefore getting lost in the process. This can occur in a variety of ways, but it requires that teachers ask themselves during every step of their lessons, "What extra support might my students need?" In Chapter Five, we'll explore this is more detail.

Examples of Scaffolding Strategies

- ◆ Asking guiding questions.
- ◆ Chunking information.
- ◆ Highlighting or color-coding steps in a project.
- ◆ Writing standards as questions for students to answer.
- ◆ Using visuals and graphic organizers such as a math graphic organizer for word problems, maps to accompany history lessons, or color coded paragraphs to help students make meaning of texts.

Ensuring Students Demonstrate Learning at High Levels

The third component of a rigorous classroom is providing each student with opportunities to demonstrate learning at high levels. A teacher recently said to me, "If we provide more challenging lessons that include extra support, then learning will happen." What I've learned is that if we want students to show us they understand what they learned at a high level, we also need to provide opportunities for students to demonstrate they have truly mastered that learning. In order for students to demonstrate their learning, they must first be engaged in academic tasks, precisely those in the classroom.

Student engagement is a critical aspect of rigor. In too many classrooms, most of the instruction consists of the teacher-centered, large-group instruction, perhaps in an interactive lecture or discussion format. The general practice during these lessons is for the teacher to ask a question and then call on a student to respond. While this provides an opportunity for one student to demonstrate understanding, the remaining students don't do so.

Another option would be for the teacher to allow all students to pair-share, respond with thumbs up or down, write their answers on small whiteboards and share their responses, or respond on handheld computers that tally the responses. Such activities hold each student accountable for demonstrating his or her understanding.

Structure of the Book

This book will provide you the tools you need to implement instructional rigor in your classroom. Each chapter is set up so that you have a short explanation of the tool, with an accompanying graphic or template if appropriate. There are a wealth of tools, please do not feel like you should implement all of them. I've designed the book so you can pick and choose which are most appropriate for your classroom and your students. You'll find examples from a variety of grade levels and subject areas, but each tool can be adapted for your use. I've organized the chapters around the acrostic RIGOR, with an additional chapter about extending your reach.

Chapters

Chapter Two: Raise Expectations Through High Standards

Chapter Three: Raise Expectations Through Questioning and Adult Behaviors

Chapter Four: Increase Depth of Instruction

Chapter Five: Give Support

Chapter Six: Options for Assessment

Chapter Seven: Reinvigorate the Environment

Chapter Eight: Extend Your Reach

In Chapters Two and Three: Raise Expectations Through High Standards, and Raise Expectations Through Questioning and Adult Behaviors, we'll be looking at the variety of ways you can put high expectations into practice. In addition to exploring an overview of the Common Core State Standards, we'll look at models for questioning and the behaviors that reinforce high expectations.

Next, in Chapter Four: Increase Depth of Instruction, we will explore a wide range of tools you can use to effectively impact your instruction. These include lesson starters, working in groups, real-life learning, and literacy across the curriculum.

Chapter Five: Give Support addresses the scaffolding needed to support students as they move to more rigorous work. Before, During, and After Lesson Strategies frame this chapter.

Chapter Six: Options for Assessment provides a range of options for assessment. We'll address types of assessment, strategies for formative assessment, homework, and grading practices.

In Chapter Seven: Reinvigorate the Environment, we turn our attention to the overall environment of your classroom. What role does the physical environment play in a rigorous classroom? What about the role of the teacher, and students' views of success and failure?

Finally, in Chapter Eight: Extend Your Reach, I'll explain ways you can truly expand the rigorous environment beyond your role. You'll see options for working with substitute teachers, parents, other teachers, and your administration.

Conclusion

I hope you will find the tools throughout the book helpful. They all are designed to meet today's rigorous standards, whether that is the Common Core or your own state's standards. Each is an effective, research-based strategy, and one that you can implement immediately in your classroom. Remember that I've provided a wide range of tools, too many to be used immediately. Please don't get overwhelmed; think of this as a true toolkit, one to return to again and again when you need a strategy for your students. I wish you the best on your journey—a journey to higher levels of learning for both you and your students. Please don't hesitate to contact me if you have any questions or if you'd like to share your successes. You can reach me at www.barbarablackburnonline.com or at bcgroup@gmail.com.

2
Raise Expectations Through High Standards

One way we can exhibit high standards is through the standards we teach. Although teachers may use different curricula, and states may use different standards, the principles remain the same.

Purpose of Standards

Why do we have standards? I overheard a teacher say, "The reason we have standards is so someone can tell us what to do." There is some truth to that; standards do guide us in what we should teach. Kay Burke (2009) explains that standards ultimately benefit students by helping educators.

Tool 1
Nine Purposes of Standards

1. Synthesize educational goals.
2. Target student achievement.
3. Align curriculum systematically.
4. Notify the public of results.
5. Determine criteria for quality work.
6. Analyze data.
7. Refocus instructional methodology.
8. Dedicate resources for professional development.
9. Serve the needs of a diverse population.

I find that five of these are particularly pertinent to our day-to-day work as teachers. Standards help us align what we are doing with the stated expectations, determine the quality of student work in relation to those expectations, and focus our instruction to best meet the standards. Additionally, by using the data provided, we can more effectively target student achievement and meet the needs of all of our students.

High Standards for Learning

Most states have moved to rigorous standards for learning. Forty-five states have moved to the Common Core State Standards, the development of which were led by the National Governors Association (NGA) and the Council of Chief State School Officers (CCSSO). However, some states have their own standards, such as Texas and Virginia. Interestingly, the standards of those states are aligned in many ways with the Common Core. Therefore, when we discuss strategies that are appropriate for meeting the Common Core Standards, they are also appropriate for states with their own standards.

Tool 2
Similarities of Texas Essentials Knowledge and Skills (TEKS) and the Common Core

Sample Commonalities of TEKS and CCSS

♦ Reading and Analyzing Multiple Texts.

♦ Providing Evidence from the Text to Support Conclusions.

♦ Focus on Academic Vocabulary.

♦ Increased Text Complexity.

♦ Focus on Problem-Solving.

♦ Use of Appropriate Tools in Math.

♦ Procedural Fluency in Math.

Source: Adapted from www.englishspanishteks.net/trainers/files/Toolbox/FAQ.pdf and www.tasmonline.net/Documents/HSCAMT2012.pdf

Tool 3
Comparison of Virginia Standards of Learning (SOL) and the Common Core

Sample Comparison of the Virginia Standards of Learning and the Common Core state Standards

English/Language Arts	Mathematics
1. The SOL begin citing sources in grade 5 with citing primary and secondary sources beginning in grade 6. The CCSS begin citing sources in grade 7 with bibliographic information.	1. The SOL strands (Number and Number Sense, Computation and Estimation, Measurement, Geometry, Probability and Statistics, and Patterns, Functions, and Algebra) remain constant throughout kindergarten—grade 8. In the CCSS document, the strand (domain) titles vary based on the content focus of that particular grade level. This flexibility in the strand content facilitates connections across the mathematics topics. The *Mathematics Curriculum Framework*, as the companion document of the SOL, rather than the SOL document itself, also makes mathematics connections, across mathematics topics.
2. Both the CCSS and SOL address grammatical conventions. The SOL address grammar, usage, and mechanics through writing, while the CCSS do the same in the Language strand.	
3. The CCSS do not prescribe a reading list per se, but they offer reading text exemplars to illustrate text complexity for each grade level. Virginia does not endorse specific titles or authors to support the SOL.	2. The SOL and CCSS utilize different organizational strands. Although the SOL strand titles are different, all concepts included mirror those of the CCSS.
4. The CCSS address the study of American literature in the 9–10 Reading Standards for Literature. Yet, the CCSS text exemplars list most American literary classics and foundational documents at grades 11–12 (e.g., *The Great Gatsby* by F. Scott Fitzgerald, *Their Eyes Were Watching God* by Zora Neale Hurston, *A Raisin in the Sun* by Lorraine Hansberry, *The Gettysburg Address* by Abraham Lincoln, *Letter from a Birmingham Jail* by Martin Luther King, Jr.).	3. By the time students complete high school mathematics SOL, they will have received at least the same mathematical content found in the CCSS, but delivered through different learning progressions.

Source: www.doe.virginia.gov/testing/common_core/index.shtml

Common Core State Standards

As stated by the authors of the Common Core, the purpose of the Common Core State Standards is to provide a consistent, clear understanding of what students are expected to learn, so teachers and parents know what they need to do to help them.

The standards are designed to be robust and relevant to the real world, reflecting the knowledge and skills that our young people need for success in college and careers. With American students fully prepared for the future, our communities will be best positioned to compete successfully in the global economy (www.core standards.org).

It's important to note that many of the shifts and areas of emphasis included in the Common Core are also included in other states' standards. As I've already mentioned, Texas and Virginia both have rigorous sets of state standards that include an emphasis on problem-solving, high levels of analysis, and informational text. Therefore, many of the suggestions in this section are also applicable to all states, not just those using the Common Core.

Tool 4
Major Shifts in the Standards

For each of the major areas of the standards, English/Language Arts, Literacy, and Math, there are significant changes. For example, in English/Language Arts, there are ten standards focusing on increased text complexity. Standard 1, deducing literal and inferred meaning from complex text, and Standard 10 reading complex text independently and proficiently serve as bookends for the other standards.

In Literacy, specific literacy-based standards are provided for both reading and writing in History/Social Studies, Science, and Technical subjects. The focus is not on these teachers becoming reading teachers; rather, they teach students to use reading and writing to access and process information in college and in the workforce.

Finally, in math, the standards stress conceptual understanding of key ideas, but they also reinforce key concepts such as place value or the laws of arithmetic to structure the concepts. Each of these three areas (English/Language Arts, Literacy, and Math) incorporates three key shifts.

Key Shifts in the Common Core

English/Language Arts Shifts	Literacy Shifts	Math Shifts
• Nonfiction for building knowledge • Reading writing speaking grounded in evidence from text • Regular practice with complex text and academic language	• Building knowledge through reading content-rich nonfiction • Reading, writing, and speaking grounded in evidence from text • Regular practice with complex text and its academic vocabulary	• Focus strongly where standards focus • Coherence think across grades and link to major topics within grades • In major topics pursue conceptual understanding procedural skill and fluency and application

Tool 5
Tiers of Vocabulary

One of the areas of emphasis in the Common Core is advanced academic vocabulary. Tiers of Vocabulary were introduced by Isabel Beck, Margaret McKeown, and Omanson in 1987.

Tier One words are acquired through everyday speech. These words are common and are typically taught at early grades or learned through everyday use around them. Tier Two includes academic words that appear across all texts. They may change meaning due to use and they present a challenge if experienced in text initially. Vocabulary instruction for these words typically adds to students' understanding of the meaning. Tier Three vocabulary is domain or content area specific. They are critical for building conceptual understanding in content, but they need to be explicit instruction. These words are best taught when they are needed in the context of the lesson.

Sample Tier Vocabulary

Tier	Examples
Tier One	Cold, cat, tired, walk, talk, look
Tier Two	Contradict, precede, retrospect, reality, mentioned
Tier Three	Chloroplasts, metamorphosed, caste, factorization, traitorous

Tool 6
Sample Tier Two Vocabulary

Tier Two Words provide an opportunity for thorough vocabulary development. These should be words that you focus on in depth, since they will have applications not only in the specified text, but across other texts and areas of the curriculum. Isabel Beck, Margaret McKeown, and Linda Kucan give us a sampling of suggested Tier Two Vocabulary for stories and novels.

Suggested Tier Two Vocabulary for Stories and Novels

Grades	Text	Suggested Tier Two Vocabulary
K-2	*Lon Po Po*: A Red-Riding Hood Story from China	Dusk, disguised, route, cunning, plump, clever, tender, paced
3-5	*Frindle*	Reputations, maximum, concentration, alert, disruption, standards, controversial, endures

see next page

Grades	Text	Suggested Tier Two Vocabulary
6-8	*A Wrinkle in Time*	Atrophied, fallible, assuaged, emanate, pungent, perplexity, jeopardize, vulnerable, distraught, reiterating, vestige
High School	*The Fall of the House of Usher*	Oppressively, pervaded, sublime, malady, acute, pallid, solace, morbid, anomalous, palpable, succumbed, paradoxical

Tool 7
Increasing Difficulty of Text

The Common Core Standards add text complexity as a dimension of literacy. To establish text complexity, the standards propose a three-pronged system:

1. Qualitative analyses of features such as levels of meaning (e.g., readers need to make inferences to understand a character's motive).

2. Reader-task variables such as readers' background knowledge of a text's topic and ways in which teachers and situations influence readers' interactions with a text (e.g., an audio of a book or the level of teacher guidance).

3. Quantitative indices such as information on the number of infrequent words and length of sentences (e.g., word indexes, sentence-length formulas, or automatic readability programs).

The standards also demand an expanded view of text materials, with a strong shift toward informational, non-fiction text. In addition to using news articles, internet source materials, and primary and secondary sources of information, teachers will need to find essays, speeches, memoirs, technical manuals, etc. You can find a full list of the recommended exemplars from the standards in Appendix B of the Common Core State Standards (www.corestandards.org/assets/Appendix_B.pdf).

Tool 8
Three Factors in Depth

When you are picking a book for use in an instructional setting, there are three aspects to consider: the qualitative and quantitative aspects of the text, and the reader-text variables.

Aspects to Consider When Choosing a Text

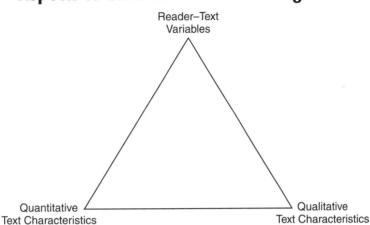

First, let's consider the text. There are quantitative factors to consider. These are the factors that readability formulas measure. We'll deal specifically with readability in the following tools. However, the quantitative factors are only the starting point in text selection.

Next, let's look at the qualitative factors in a text. What factors affect the quantitative readability of the text? For example, we should think about the text support features. Are there supporting features within the text that help the reader? These might be pictures, charts, graphs or headings that help organize the reading. It also includes the print size, which makes a text easier or harder to read. Then, we should consider the quality of the text. What is the overall quality of the book? Is it lively and engaging? Is it of enduring literary quality? Finally, are there deeper levels of meaning within the text? For example, are there literary allusions? A student might be able to read *The Old Man and the Sea*, but would think it is a book about an old man and a fish. Understanding the metaphorical nature of the book is a qualitative piece of evaluation.

Lastly, there are reader-task factors. For the task itself, there are several items to consider.

For what purpose is this particular book to be used?

♦ Are you looking for a book to read aloud or provide via audio to students? If so, pick a book that is more difficult than the students' reading level, since their listening vocabulary is typically higher that their reading vocabulary.

♦ Are you looking for a book for instruction where you plan to provide support? You might choose a book at, or close to, their reading level, since 75 percent accuracy and comprehension at their instructional level.

♦ Are you looking for a book for fluent reading, where students independently read a book with 90 percent accuracy for added confidence and fluency? Then, choose a book below their reading level.

♦ In the case of self-selection of books, are you looking for a book for information or pleasure? Usually, you pick an easier book for pleasure.

Next the **reader** brings a variety of important factors to the reading experience. There are four important areas to consider:

+ *Reading ability*, which can be measured in a variety of ways. This helps you understand how much support will be needed for the student to read the text.

+ *Prior knowledge* is the student's background knowledge about the subject. A lack of prior knowledge can negatively affect the reading experience.

+ *Interest level* determines reader commitment. If the reader is totally uninterested in the subject of the book, nothing else really seems to matter, especially to the reader.

+ Finally, *developmental appropriateness* is an important concept. For example, a fifth grader may possess the ability to read *Silas Marner*, but, from a developmental appropriateness view, that book may not be the best choice for that student. Conversely, an older student with limited reading abilities is often turned off by books that he or she is able to read, but that they perceive as too childish.

All the factors within the major areas are important considerations when evaluating the appropriateness of a text for a reader. Now let's look at the quantitative considerations, or readability formulas.

Tool 9
The Lexile Framework

For our purposes today, let's look in more depth at the original readability formula recommended by the CCSS. The Lexile Framework is one tool for looking at a reader's ability in relation to the difficulty of text. It is a tool, a knowledge base that can enhance reading methods and sharpen the focus of instructional programs currently in use in a school or district. Used in conjunction with an educator's professional judgment, the Lexile Framework provides:

+ A way to define (with books and other text materials) what is above grade level, on grade level, and below grade level, according to the standardized test used.

+ A way to understand a student's location on the reading spectrum, based on their performance on a standardized test or informal assessment.

+ A way to align classroom libraries, resource materials, textbooks, and library materials to standardized tests such as MAPS.

The Lexile level is based on two factors: sentence length and word frequency. Generally easier text has shorter sentences and words that are used frequently in our language; harder text has longer, more complicated sentences and words that are less frequently used.

Lexile Thermometer of Text Complexity

Lexile

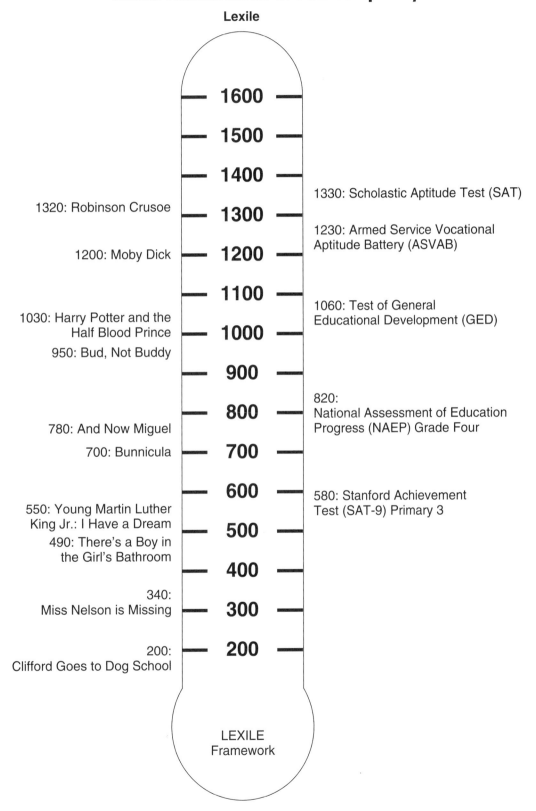

1320: Robinson Crusoe — **1300** —

1200: Moby Dick — **1200** —

1030: Harry Potter and the
Half Blood Prince — **1000** —
950: Bud, Not Buddy

— **900** —

— **800** —
780: And Now Miguel

700: Bunnicula — **700** —

— **600** —

550: Young Martin Luther
King Jr.: I Have a Dream
490: There's a Boy in — **500** —
the Girl's Bathroom

— **400** —

340:
Miss Nelson is Missing — **300** —

200: — **200** —
Clifford Goes to Dog School

1330: Scholastic Aptitude Test (SAT)

1230: Armed Service Vocational
Aptitude Battery (ASVAB)

1060: Test of General
Educational Development (GED)

820:
National Assessment of Education
Progress (NAEP) Grade Four

580: Stanford Achievement
Test (SAT-9) Primary 3

LEXILE
Framework

By searching for titles, authors, topics, or by numerical range on www.lexile.com, you can create book lists for students based on their current reading levels or to match the recommended range for your grade level. Searching for books is free; other testing and support materials from publishers are available for purchase.

Sample Books by Gary Paulsen

Title	Lexile
Legend of Red Horse Cavern	470
Captive	600
Grizzly	720
Dogsong	930
Hatchet	1020
Brian's Winter	1140

Tool 10
Other Readability Formulas

There are other readability formulas also recommended in the Common Core State Standards. They work similarly to Lexiles. ATOS is the readability formula used by Accelerated Reader. Part of a purchased program, it provides both testing to place students and numerical indicators of difficulty for books. There are sources for some published levels, although they are limited.

The Degrees of Reading Power® (DRP®) Program provides a holistic, criterion-referenced measure of how well students process and understand increasingly more complex text. It is also a purchased program, although you may be able to find published levels from a variety of sources.

There are several other common readability formulas. For example, you can cut and paste text into Microsoft Word and obtain a readability level. Additionally, using the advanced search, Google will return results to you by readability level. However, keep in mind that, at the publication date of this book, none of these are used as exemplars in the Common Core.

Tool 11
Increased Difficulty of Text Levels

You may have used one or more of these readability formulas in the past. However, based on the Common Core, the expected level of text difficulty students should read is higher. For example, look at how the expected Lexile levels increase with the Common Core.

Shifts in Lexile Levels

Text Complexity Grade Band in the Standards	Old Lexile Ranges	Lexile Ranges Aligned to CCR expectations
K–1	N/A	N/A
2–3	450–725	450–790
4–5	645–845	770–980
6–8	860–1010	955–1155
9–10	960–1115	1080–1305
11–CCR	1070–1220	1215–1355

Tool 12
Close Reading

When I was teaching, my students and I had two different versions of closely reading a text. Mine involved analysis and thought; theirs focused on finishing as quickly as possible. The goal of close reading is a deeper understanding of the text. It involves making observations and interpreting your observations.

Patricia Kain at Harvard University provides a description of the process of making observations for close reading.

Making Observations for Close Reading

1. *Read with a pencil in hand, and annotate the text.*

   "Annotating" means underlining or highlighting key words and phrases—anything that strikes you as surprising or significant, or that raises questions—as well as making notes in the margins. When we respond to a text in this way, we not only force ourselves to pay close attention, but we also begin to think with the author about the evidence—the first step in moving from reader to writer.

2. *Look for patterns in the things you've noticed about the text—repetitions, contradictions, similarities.*

3. *Ask questions about the patterns you've noticed—especially how and why.*

Source: http://writingcenter.fas.harvard.edu/pages/how-do-close-reading>

Tool 13
Teaching Students to Annotate Text

It's important to teach students how to annotate text materials. First, choose a short text, and model what you want students to do. Then, using another short section of text, ask students to look for several specific aspects of annotation. Then, pair students so they can annotate a text together. After another class discussion, provide the opportunity for them to practice independently. As with any strategy, students will improve with quality practice.

Carol Porter (2004) provides sample prompts for students to use before, during, and after reading. Although these are geared for novels and short stories, they can be easily adapted for informational text sources. I'd also recommend you create a bookmark with selected prompts for students to have as a handy reference.

Annotating Text

Before reading

♦ Examine the front and back covers (books).
♦ Read the title and any subtitles.
♦ Examine the illustrations.
♦ Examine the print (bold, italics, etc.).
♦ Examine the way the text is set up (book, short story, diary, dialogue, article, etc.).

   As you examine and read these, write questions, and make predictions and/or connections near these parts of the text.

During reading
Mark these things in the text:
♦ Characters (who).
♦ When (setting).
♦ Where (setting).
♦ Vocabulary.
♦ Important information.
Write in the margins:
♦ Summarize.
♦ Make predictions.
♦ Formulate opinions.
♦ Make connections.

Ask questions
♦ Analyze the author's craft.
♦ Write reflections/reactions/comments.
♦ Look for patterns/repetitions.

After reading

♦ Reread annotations—draw conclusions.

♦ Reread introduction and conclusion—try to figure out something new.

♦ Examine patterns/repetitions—determine possible meaning.

♦ Determine what the title might mean.

Use the "After Reading" strategies to write a notebook entry.

Source: http://vd-p.d91.k12.id.us/Curriculum_Resources/Sheltered%20Instruction%20(SIOP)/Fall%202011%20Class%20-%20Where%20Every%20Student%20Learns/Session%2001/Fall%202011/01_Beyond%20the%20Yellow%20Highlighter.pdf

Tool 14
Essential Skills for Close Reading

Sunday Cummins provides a list of six essential skills for close reading.

1. Tapping prior knowledge related to text structure.
2. Tapping prior topical and vocabulary knowledge.
3. Setting a purpose.
4. Self-monitoring for meaning.
5. Determining what is important.
6. Synthesizing.

This provides a useful view because it specifies all the skills students need to utilize to accomplish close readings. Each is important, yet we cannot assume students know how to do theses. It is critical that we teach and model each of the strategies.

Tool 15
The Role of Pre-Reading in Close Reading

I'm often asked by teachers, "What am I supposed to do for pre-reading? Don't the standards say just throw students into the text?" There is a difference between explaining everything students will be reading beforehand, and just supporting students by providing critical information and prior knowledge for those who need it.

For example, if we want students to discover information in the text, telling them everything about the plot in advance spoils the reading experience for them. So what does this mean? We need to be strategic in our choices as to what we do with students prior to the text. Timothy Shanahan (www.shanahanonliteracy.com) recommends that pre-reading should be brief compared to the length of time of the reading itself. He also suggests that teachers not reveal info students can gain by themselves; rather, they should give students a reason to read and/or arouse curiosity.

Tool 16
Close Reading and Informational Texts

What does close reading look like in an informational text? Sunday Cummins in her book, Close Reading of Informational Texts, suggests two areas of focus:

1. Read closely to determine what the text says explicitly and to make logical inferences from it; cite specific textual evidence when writing or speaking to support conclusions drawn from the text.

2. Determine central ideas or themes of a text and analyze their development; summarize the key supporting details and ideas.

In my social studies class, this meant that students needed to pay attention to what the text actually said, which was sometimes different from what they thought they read. For example, with close reading, not only do we want students to pay attention to the explicit meaning of the text, we want their conclusions and inferences to be based on that explicit information. As a part of that, students should be able to cite specific information to back up any responses, written or verbal.

Tool 17
Reading Standards and Informational Text

The focus on informational text in the CCSS supports the expectation of college/career readiness. A tremendous amount of the reading and writing students will do after high school is informational, rather than fiction. This requires students to demonstrate their understanding in a variety of ways. For example, let's look at sample reading standards related to informational text for grades 3, 5, and 8 to see the progression of the standards.

Sample Informational Reading Standards

Grade 3	Grade 5	Grade 8
Ask and answer questions to demonstrate understanding of a text, referring explicitly to the text as the basis for the answers.	Quote accurately from a text when explaining what the text says explicitly and when drawing inferences from the text.	Cite the textual evidence that most strongly supports an analysis of what the text says explicitly as well as inferences drawn from the text.

Grade 3	Grade 5	Grade 8
Determine the main idea of a text; recount the key details and explain how they support the main idea.	Determine two or more main ideas of a text and explain how they are supported by key details; summarize the text.	Determine a central idea of a text and analyze its development over the course of the text, including its relationship to supporting ideas; provide an objective summary of the text.

Tool 18
Sample Sources for Close Reading

Although almost any text can be used for close reading, there are some sample sources that can be particularly helpful. For example, the *New York Times* publishes "Room for Debate", in which guest columnists present views on key issues. *Achieve the Core* (www.achievethecore.org/ela-literacy-common-core/sample-lessons/close-reading-exemplars/) provides sample lessons with close reading exemplars. And Kelly Gallagher gives texts he uses in his classroom in his articles of the week (http://kellygallagher.org/resources/articles.html). You may also want to refer to the list of exemplars provided in the Common Core State Standards.

Tool 19
Close Reading and Non-Print

Close reading can also occur in non-print sources. For example, William Kist points out that one can compare and contrast a story, drama, or poem to its audio, filmed, staged, or multimedia version, analyzing the effects of techniques unique to each medium (lighting, sound, etc.). You can also evaluate the advantages and disadvantages of using different mediums such as print, digital text, video, or multimedia to present a particular topic or idea. He provides a set of prompts for close reading that are valuable to consider:

Prompts for Close Reading of Nonprint and Print Text (describe details)

Film Clip	Lighting, Editing, Short Composition, Costuming Set Design, Sound Effects
Visual Art	Composition, Color, Light, Point of View, Brush Strokes
Music	Instrumentation, Tempo, Rhythm, Dynamics, Intensity
Print Text	Literary Allusion, Character, Dialogue, Descriptive Words, Length of Sentences

When comparing to informational print text, you could use prompts such as the point of view of the author, arguments presented, and applicable evidence.

Tool 20
Writing and the Common Core

There are ten writing standards for each grade level. You'll find emphasis on strong connections to reading, informative and explanatory writing about complex ideas and information, argumentative writing rather than persuasive writing, using technology for research and to produce or publish work, and on the overall process of writing. In other words, students will read complex texts, write and rewrite about analysis from an argumentative point of view, and produce their work using technology.

Tool 21
Writing Standards and Sample Activities

Let's look at the ten writing standards and how the relate to your classroom. The writing standards can be used in any classroom, grade level, or subject area. Below, you'll see the writing standards, as well as sample activities for each standard.

Sample Writing Activities That Meet the Standards

Writing Anchor Standard	Sample Activities
Write arguments to support claims in an analysis of substantive topics or texts, using valid reasoning and relevant and sufficient evidence.	Debates Three-Minute Argument Blog Entries
Write informative/explanatory texts to examine and convey complex ideas and information clearly and accurately through the effective selection, organization, and analysis of content.	Source Summaries Venture Capitalist Proposal for Idea Information Guide on Topic
Write narratives to develop real or imagined experiences or events using effective technique, well-chosen details, and well-structured event sequences.	Describe Real or Hypothetical Job Interview. Choose one event leading up to World War Two. Explain the event and its importance. Describe your ideal classroom.

see next page

Writing Anchor Standard	Sample Activities
Produce clear and coherent writing in which the development, organization, and style are appropriate to task, purpose, and audience.	Create a plan to present to your principal for improving your school. Write a list of questions (and responses) for an interview with a historic figure. Write a set of instructions on how to create a PowerPoint presentation.
Develop and strengthen writing as needed by planning, revising, editing, rewriting, or trying a new approach.	Using a self-reflection guide, revise your writing. Using perspective questions provided by the teacher, revise your work by trying a new approach. Work with a partner and use the peer review guide to provide feedback to each other.
Use Technology, including the Internet, to produce and publish writing and to interact and collaborate with others.	Create a video blogs Create webquests Upload presentation to a cloud-based service for group revisions, then present to the class.
Conduct short as well as more sustained research projects based on focused questions, demonstrating understanding of the subject under investigation.	Complete a webquest designed by the teacher. Research a specific topic using 3–5 sources. Compare a primary and secondary source on a topic.
Gather relevant information from multiple print and digital resources, assess the credibility and accuracy of each source, and integrate the information while avoiding plagiarism.	Compare a Wikipedia article to at least three other sources. Provide documentation as to the accuracy of the Wikipedia article. Choose a fiction story and an accompanying nonfiction text (such as a story about alligators and an article about alligators). How accurate is the fictional story? Choose an internet source. Assess it using the Tips for Evaluating Internet Sources (see Tool 22).
Draw evidence from literary or informational texts to support analysis, reflection, and research.	Develop a problem/solution paper. Research the topic of your choice, using four to six sources. Debate a side of an argument, supporting your points with multiple references.
Write routinely over extended time frames (time for research, reflection, and revision) and shorter time frames (a single sitting or a day or two) for a range of tasks, purposes, and audiences.	Incorporate writing throughout your instruction on a daily basis.

Tool 22
Tips for Evaluating Internet Sources

In writing anchor standard 8, "Gather relevant information from multiple print and digital resources, assess the credibility and accuracy of each source, and integrate the information while avoiding plagiarism," students are expected to assess internet sources. My niece and nephew surf the web regularly for research and homework, but they assume any site they find is credible and accurate. We must teach students how to evaluate all sources, but particularly internet sources. The tips below can help guide students' thinking.

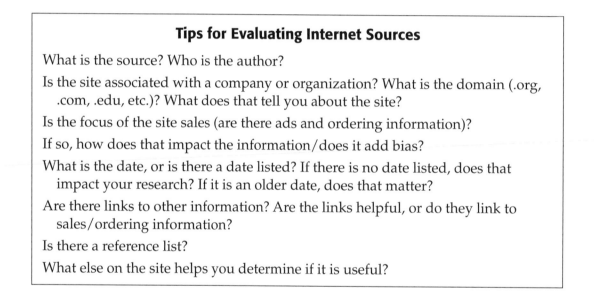

Tips for Evaluating Internet Sources

What is the source? Who is the author?

Is the site associated with a company or organization? What is the domain (.org, .com, .edu, etc.)? What does that tell you about the site?

Is the focus of the site sales (are there ads and ordering information)?

If so, how does that impact the information/does it add bias?

What is the date, or is there a date listed? If there is no date listed, does that impact your research? If it is an older date, does that matter?

Are there links to other information? Are the links helpful, or do they link to sales/ordering information?

Is there a reference list?

What else on the site helps you determine if it is useful?

More on the Common Core

Now that we've looked at some big issues that affect subjects across all areas of the curriculum, let's turn our attention to some specialized topics.

Specialized Topics

Mathematical Practice Standards

English/Language Arts Standards: Grammar

Technology in the Common Core

The Common Core and English Language Learners

The Common Core for Students with Special Needs

Tool 23
Math Practice Standards

One of the challenges in math instruction is the need to balance mathematical content with skills such as problem-solving and reasoning. With the new Common Core, there are specific content standards such as number sense, but there are also eight standards for mathematical practice.

Eight Standards for Mathematical Practice

1. Make sense of problems and persevere in solving them.
2. Reason abstractly and quantitatively.
3. Construct viable arguments and critique the reasoning of others.
4. Model with mathematics.
5. Use appropriate tools strategically.
6. Attend to precision.
7. Look for and make use of structure.
8. Look for and express regularity in repeated reasoning.

Source: Common Core State Standards Initiative, 2012

Tool 24
The Doorway to the Mathematical Practice Standards

Teaching the mathematical practice standards does not negate the importance of content standards; however, it raises the level of focus on the practices of math, pointing out that it's not enough to compute if a student can't use that skill strategically.

According to Leslie Texas and Tammy Jones, The Standards for Mathematical Practice (SMP) can be seen as the doorway to implementing the Common Core State Standards for Mathematics. The purpose of developing strategies to support the implementation of the CCSSM, the SMP can be grouped as shown in the doorway graphic.

A door cannot function without a frame. The frame is the support system that holds the door in place. The two SMP that serve as the frame of the door are the following:

1. Make sense of problems and persevere in solving them.
5. Use appropriate tools strategically.

The threshold is another integral part of a door. The function of the threshold is to provide a transition between the inside and the outside or between rooms. SMP #6, "Attend **to precision**," serves as the threshold for the SMP doorway to the CCSSM. It is through precise and effective communication that students are able to gain insights

Doorway Analogy for Understanding the Math Requirements

Standards for Mathematical Practice

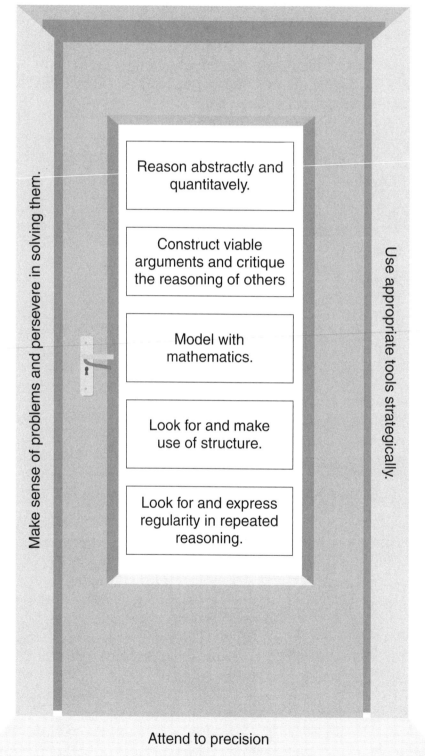

From Texas and Jones, *Strategies for Common Core Mathematics, 6-8*

about how they think about mathematics. As the National Council of Teachers of Mathematics (NCTM) states in *PSSM*, "It is important to give students experiences that help them appreciate the power and precision of mathematical language" (2005, p. 63).

The key to unlocking the door of the SMP is being deliberate and intentional in their implementation. It is one thing to say the SMPs are embedded in daily instruction. It is another to actually seamlessly interweave the mathematical practices with content instruction.

Tool 25
Sample Standards for Mathematical Practice with Activities

To better understand the SMPs, below you will find sample activities for several of the standards of mathematical practice.

Sample Standards with Explanation of Possible Activity

Standard for Mathematical Practice	Explanation	Example (when it applies)
CCSS.Math. Practice. MP1 Make sense of problems and persevere in solving them.	Provide the students with a list of question prompts to use to solve problems. A fun activity would be to use a book mark similar to those used when reading books, with the questions written to help students remember what to ask themselves. • What tools do I need to help me solve this problem? • What answer did I get on the calculator? • What is my pencil/paper answer? • Is my answer sensible? • My answer does not match the one in the book, where is my mistake? • Did I review my response(s) before moving to the next problem? • Where can I look in the book to give me some hints on how to solve this problem?	**CCSS.Math.Content.1.MD.A.1** Order three objects by length; compare the lengths of two objects indirectly by using a third object. **Probing questions** • Which object should I use to check the length of the others? Is my answer correct? Yes, No, I do not know. • If yes, I may move on to the next problem. • If no, I must recheck my answer. • What if I don't know? Ask a friend, measure the objects, ask the teacher? Depending on the students, the teacher may not provide all the prompts.

see next page

Standard for Mathematical Practice	Explanation	Example (when it applies)
CCSS.Math.Practice.MP3 Construct viable arguments and critique the reasoning of others.	Allow students to work with partners or in a group to work on problems. Encourage the students to explore at least two ways to solve the problem and discuss which way they think is best and support their argument with mathematical facts.	**CCSS.Math.Content.6.EE.B.5** Understand solving an equation or inequality as a process of answering a question: which values from a specified set, if any, make the equation or inequality true? Use substitution to determine whether a given number in a specified set makes an equation or inequality true.
		What value of x will make this equation true? With your partner, come up with two ways to solve this problem. Share which you think is easier and explain why. You don't have to agree on a method. X + 15 = 20
CCSS.Math.Practice.MP5 Use appropriate tools strategically.	Provide students tools to assist in solving problems such as calculators, computer software, tablet apps or concrete objects. Dont forget pencil and paper. Give the students a choice of using at least two tools and require them to explain why they chose those tools and if they had to use a different one once they started the work, explain why they made the change.	**CCSS.Math.Content.HSF-LE.A.2** Construct linear and exponential functions, including arithmetic and geometric sequences, given a graph, a description of a relationship, or two input-output pairs (include reading these from a table). A student may chosen pencil/paper and calculator but there are other options available like the *Functions App* by Learn It Applications for the IPAD.

Note: Columns one and three are taken directly from the standards.

Tool 26
Teaching Grammar in the Common Core

In the Common Core, although grammar is addressed with separate standards, it is expected that grammar instruction is embedded within the other English/Language Arts standards. This is important, because when we teach grammar in isolation, students likely do not have a full understanding of the concepts, and they don't remember them or apply them in their writing. In the standards, grammar is linked to texts and their own writing. Sean Ruday provides five ~~ing grammar into your instruction.

Five Recommendations for Teac~

1. Show students examples of grammatical concep~
2. Discuss how the authors of those works use gr~ enhance their writing.
3. Discuss how the literary works would look if tho~~ ~ not used.
4. Ask students to use specific grammatical concepts in their own writing.
5. Ask students to reflect on how those grammatical concepts enhance their works.

Tool 27
Integration of Technology and the Common Core

I was recently asked why Instructional Technology Standards were not written for the Common Core. The answer is simple. Technology is integrated throughout the standards, and are an expected part of instruction. Throughout the standards, you'll find references to different mediums; diverse formats and media; and specifically digital media. For example, you will find references to technology in the writing standards (see Tool 21).

What the Common Core State Standards Say About Technology

"To be ready for college, workforce training, and life in a technological society, students need the ability to gather, comprehend, evaluate, synthesize, and report on information and ideas, to conduct original research in order to answer questions or solve problems, and to analyze and create a high volume and extensive range of print and nonprint texts in media forms old and new."

"The need to conduct research and to produce and consume media is embedded into every aspect of today's curriculum. In like fashion, research and media skills and understandings are embedded throughout the Standards rather than treated in a separate section."

"Students who are college and career ready employ technology thoughtfully to enhance their reading, writing, speaking, listening, and language use. They tailor their searches online to acquire useful information efficiently, and they integrate what they learn using technology with what they learn offline. They are familiar with the strengths and limitations of various technological tools and mediums and can select and use those best suited to their communication goals."

"When making mathematical models, [students] know that technology can enable them to visualize the results of varying assumptions, explore consequences, and compare predictions with data. Mathematically proficient students at various grade levels are able to identify relevant external mathematical resources, such as digital content located on a website, and use them to pose or solve problems. They are able to use technological tools to explore and deepen their understanding of concepts."

30

...heick (2013) shows how thinking verbs can be achieved through technology. ...vided additional examples within his recommendations.

> Publishing; whether through a blog, photo blog, or video blog, requires consideration of audience, purpose, structure, text features, and format. Create mathematical models using a variety of technology.
>
> Collaboration requires that a student plan, adopt, adapt, rethink, and revise. Apps and social media can support this area, particularly the use of wikis for group work.
>
> Evaluation is not just a comparison; students can demonstrate a preference for social media such as twitter or tumblr by evaluating pros and cons of each.

Tool 28
English/Language Arts Research Recommendations from the Common Core for English Language Learners (ELS)

The Common Core Standards are abundantly clear that English Language Learners (ELLs) should be held to the high expectations of the standards. However, you may need to provide extra time and support to ensure their success. In the standards, the authors provide research-based recommendations for working with ELLs in both English/Language Arts and Mathematics. These recommendations are helpful as you plan to adjust instruction as needed.

English/Language Arts Research Recommendations

- Literacy-rich school environments where students are immersed in a variety of language experiences.
- Instruction that develops foundational skills in English and enables ELLs to participate fully in grade-level coursework.
- Coursework that prepares ELLs for postsecondary education or the workplace, yet is made comprehensible for students learning content in a second language (through specific pedagogical techniques and additional resources).
- Opportunities for classroom discourse and interaction that are well-designed to enable ELLs to develop communicative strengths in language arts.
- Ongoing assessment and feedback to guide learning.
- Speakers of English who know the language well enough to provide ELLs with models and support.

Source: www.corestandards.org/assets/application-for-english-learners.pdf

Tool 29
Mathematics Research Recommendations from the Common Core for English Language Learners

Mathematical Research Recommendations

♦ Language switching can be swift, highly automatic, and facilitate rather than inhibit solving word problems in the second language, as long as the student's language proficiency is sufficient for understanding the text of the word problem.

♦ Instruction should ensure that students understand the text of word problems before they attempt to solve them.

♦ Instruction should include a focus on "mathematical discourse" and "academic language" because these are important for ELLs. Although it is critical that students who are learning English have opportunities to communicate mathematically, this is not primarily a matter of learning vocabulary. Students learn to participate in mathematical reasoning, not by learning vocabulary, but by making conjectures, presenting explanations, and/or constructing arguments.

♦ While vocabulary instruction is important, it is not sufficient for supporting mathematical communication. Furthermore, vocabulary drill and practice are not the most effective instructional practices for learning vocabulary. Research has demonstrated that vocabulary learning occurs most successfully through instructional environments that are language-rich, actively involve students in using language, require that students both understand spoken or written words and also express that understanding orally and in writing, and require students to use words in multiple ways over extended periods of time. To develop written and oral communication skills, students need to participate in negotiating meaning for mathematical situations and in mathematical practices that require output from students.

Source: www.corestandards.org/assets/application-for-english-learners.pdf

Tool 30
Five Strategies for the Common Core for English Language Learners

As we've already discussed, in the Common Core, English Language Learners are expected to work at same level of expectations. However, they will likely need additional time and support, along with close monitoring.

Paul Boyd-Bastone suggests five strategies to help beginning ELLs meet the Common Core.

Five Strategies to Help Beginning ELLs Meet the Common Core

1. Employ simple "caretaker" speech. Slow down, emphasize key words, use calming low volume voice, emphasis on key words.

2. Use realia and visuals (real objects and pictures, diagrams, and models critical or material may not be comprehended).

3. Show meaning with gestures and Total Physical Response. TPR Teacher models actions and students then act out directions, then students repeat directions if possible.

4. Avoid forced speech. Don't say "Speak English" expecting that. Beginners may need to discuss in native language to show deeper understanding.

5. Select attractive books and read with students (well-illustrated); comprehensible.

Another strategy that is particularly effective is layering meaning (see Tool 121 in Chapter Five). This is especially applicable to ELLs, who may struggle with the more difficult text due to the specialized vocabulary.

Tool 31
Sample Unit for English Language Learners

In *Education Week*, Lesli Maxwell describes an ELA unit developed by a team of ELL experts on art of persuasion incorporating complex info text and argumentative writing to be used with ELL students in grades seven or eight. The lessons incorporate text, multimedia, and interactive activities. Many of the speeches are viewed rather than read.

Sample Lessons for ELLs on the Art of Persuasion

Lesson	Topic/Focus	Text(s)
Lesson 1	Advertising in the Contemporary World: An Introduction to Persuasive Texts	Can You Live with Dirty Water (Canadian TV spot)
Lesson 2	Persuasion in Historical Context	Gettysburg Address (Abraham Lincoln)
Lesson 3	Ethos, Logos, and Pathos in Civil Rights Movement Speeches	I Have a Dream (Martin Luther King, Jr.) On the Death of Martin Luther King (Robert Kennedy) The Civil Rights Movement: Fraud, Sham, and Hoax (George Wallace)

see next page

Lesson	Topic/Focus	Text(s)
Lesson 4	Persuasion as Text: Organizational, Grammatical, and Lexical Moves	All Together Now, Barbara Jordan
Lesson 5	Putting it Together: Analyzing and Producing Persuasive Text	The Girl Who Silenced the World for Five Minutes (Severn Suzuki)

Tool 32
The Common Core for Students with Special Needs

The CCSS are applicable to students with special needs. In fact, a key point within the standards is that "students with disabilities—students eligible under the Individuals with Disabilities Education Act (IDEA)—must be challenged to excel within the general curriculum and be prepared for success in their post-school lives, including college and/or careers."

Tool 33
Support for Students with Special Needs

The Common Core calls for instruction for students with special needs to incorporate both support and accommodations. These should include:

♦ Supports and related services.

♦ An Individualized Education Program (IEP).

♦ Qualified and Prepared teachers and specialized instructional support personnel.

Also, in order to be successful with the CCSS, students may be provided with three additional supports and services.

1. Instructional supports for learning by presenting information in multiple ways.
2. Instructional accommodations which do not change the standards.
3. Assistive technology devices and services.

Tool 34
Sample Accommodations

Accommodations are changes that can be made to the way students with disabilities are instructed and assessed. Many of these are changes you may already use with students who are struggling in your class.

Accommodations

Extra wait time

Procedures clarification

Minimizing classroom distractions

Homework reminders and planners

Increased one-to-one assistance

Classroom signals for attention

Visual organizer

Scribe or note taker

Guided notes

Shortened assignments (if all learning objectives are still covered)

Breaking lengthy assignments into chunks

Tool 35
Universal Design for Learning

Universal Design for Learning (UDL) is included in the Common Core in the section labeled "applications for students with disabilities." It is considered a guide for working, not only with special needs students, but the principles are applicable to all students. This makes it particularly helpful in classrooms utilizing the inclusion model.

UDL differs from the standards themselves in that it addresses how teachers design instruction, how students engage in learning, as well as how students demonstrate learning. Under UDL, students are still engaging in rigorous work, just with some changes in instruction.

The National Center on Universal Design for Learning provides a one page overview that explains the principles and actions of UDL in a simple manner.

Universal Design for Learning Guidelines

I. Provide Multiple Means of **Representation**	II. Provide Multiple Means of **Action and Expression**	III. Provide Multiple Means of **Engagement**
1: Provide options for perception	4: Provide options for physical action	7: Provide options for recruiting interest
1.1 Offer ways of customizing the display of information	4.1 Vary the methods for response and navigation	7.1 Optimize individual choice and autonomy
1.2 Offer alternatives for auditory information	4.2 Optimize access to tools and assistive technologies	7.2 Optimize relevance, value, and authenticity
1.3 Offer alternatives for visual information		7.3 Minimize threats and distractions
2: Provide options for language, mathematical expressions, and symbols	5: Provide options for expression and communication	8: Provide options for sustaining effort and persistence
2.1 Clarify vocabulary and symbols	5.1 Use multiple media for communication	8.1 Heighten salience of goals and objectives
2.2 Clarify syntax and structure	5.2 Use multiple tools for construction and composition	8.2 Vary demands and resources to optimize challenge
2.3 Support decoding of text, mathematical notation, and symbols	5.3 Build fluencies with graduated levels of support for practice and performance	8.3 Foster collaboration and community
2.4 Promote understanding across languages		8.4 Increase mastery-oriented feedback
2.5 Illustrate through multiple media		
3: Provide options for comprehension	6: Provide options for executive functions	9: Provide options for self-regulation
3.1 Activate or supply background knowledge	6.1 Guide appropriate goal-setting	9.1 Promote expectations and beliefs that optimize motivation
3.2 Highlight patterns, critical features, big ideas, and relationships	6.2 Support planning and strategy development	9.2 Facilitate personal coping skills and strategies
3.3 Guide information processing, visualization, and manipulation	6.3 Facilitate managing information and resources	9.3 Develop self-assessment and reflection
3.4 Maximize transfer and generalization	6.4 Enhance capacity for monitoring progress	
Resourceful, knowledgeable learners	**Strategic, goal-directed learners**	**Purposeful, motivated learners**

Conclusion

Starting points for raising expectations are our curriculum and standards. Each provides high benchmarks for students, and we know that with our help, students rise to the level of expectations provided.

Reflection into Action

1. What are three main tools from this chapter you could use in your classroom?

2. Which of those three will you put into place in the next three days?

3. Are there any resources you need to make this happen?

4. Which one would you like to implement next week?

5. What other tools do you want to consider for the future?

6. Is there anything else from this chapter you want to remember after you finish the book?

3
Raise Expectations Through Questioning and Adult Behaviors

The Pygmalion Effect, named after the play by George Bernard Shaw, states that people respond to the expectations placed upon them. For example, if we expect students to perform at high levels, they do. Conversely, if we have low expectations, they tend to prove that we are right to believe so. In this chapter, we'll focus on two ways to raise expectations: questioning strategies and adult behaviors.

Questioning

Our questioning strategies reflect our high expectations. When we ask students higher order questions, we are showing them we expect them to answer at higher levels. On the other hand, when we only ask students recall questions such as "Who did this"? we are demonstrating that we don't really expect them to know any more than the most basic answers.

There are multiple models for questioning available to you. In order to provide the fullest understanding of the concept of higher order questioning, we'll look at eight models. We'll begin with the classic Bloom's Taxonomy, move to Webb's Depth of Knowledge, which is incorporated into the Common Core and other rigorous state standards, and then look at six other designs.

Questioning Models
Bloom's Taxonomy
Webb's Depth of Knowledge
Cognitive Rigor Matrix

Costa's House of Questions
QUILT Model of Questioning
Marzano's Five Dimensions of Thinking
Essential Questions
Socratic Questioning
Effective Questions

Tool 36
Bloom's Taxonomy

The original Bloom's Taxonomy of Educational Objectives, released in 1956, was designed to help teachers write objectives and create tests to address a variety of levels of understanding. In 2001, a group of researchers revised the original taxonomy to include a more rigorous progression.

By using the verbs and descriptors, you can plan objectives, activities, and assessments that allow students to learn different types of knowledge using a variety of processes. The widely used revised taxonomy is a complex but useful method for addressing all levels of questioning.

Sample Questions Based on Bloom's Taxonomy

Level	Description	Sample Question
Remember	Retrieve knowledge, recognize, recall, locate, or identify.	Identify the villain in the story.
Understand	Clarify, paraphrase, illustrate, classify, categorize, summarize, predict, compare/contrast.	Summarize the characters' encounter with the villain.
Apply	Apply to a familiar or unfamiliar task.	Choose your favorite scene and apply it to a real-life situation.
Analyze	Determine how parts relate, organize/outline, differentiate between relevant and irrelevant material.	Identify the three major plot points, providing evidence as to why those are the most relevant.
Evaluate	Make judgments based on evidence, judge, critique.	Critique the actions of the villain.
Create	Generate, hypothesize, plan, produce	Generate an alternative ending.

Note: You'll find more on Bloom's questioning in Chapter 6: Options for Assessment.

Tool 37
Planning Tool for Bloom's Taxonomy

Rebecca Stobaugh provides a Cognitive Domain Planning Tool to assist as you plan instruction and assessment for different aspects of Bloom's Taxonomy.

Cognitive Domain Planning Tool

Process Categories	Instructional Tasks	Formative Assessments	Summative Assessments
Remember			
1.1 Recognizing			
1.2 Recalling			
Understand			
2.1 Interpreting			
2.2 Exemplifying			
2.3 Classifying			
2.4 Summarizing			
2.5 Inferring			
2.6 Comparing			
2.7 Explaining			
Apply			
3.1 Executing			
3.2 Implementing			
Analyze			
4.1 Differentiating			
4.2 Organizing			
4.3 Attributing			
Evaluate			
5.1 Checking			
5.2 Critiquing			

see next page

Process Categories	Instructional Tasks	Formative Assessments	Summative Assessments
Create			
6.1 Generating			
6.2 Planning			
6.3 Producing			

From Stobaugh, *Assessing Critical Thinking in Middle and High Schools*

Tool 38
Webb's Depth of Knowledge

In contrast to Bloom's Taxonomy, Webb's Depth of Knowledge (DOK) focuses on complexity rather than the difficulty level of the task. It is more complicated to understand because you can't just consider the verbs—they are not sufficient on their own to truly demonstrate the complexity of the task, the prior knowledge needed to complete the task, and the cognitive processes needed to be successful.

Since Webb's DOK is an integral part of the Common Core State Standards, it is important to fully understand their meanings. When I spoke with Norman Webb's assistant via email, he directed me to the full meaning of each level and suggested I use those rather than some of the simplified visuals that are available on the Internet. Let's take a look at each.

Webb's Depth of Knowledge

Level One	Level Two
Level 1 (Recall) includes the recall of information such as a fact, definition, term, or a simple procedure, as well as performing a simple algorithm or applying a formula. That is, in mathematics a one-step, well-defined, and straight algorithmic procedure should be included at this lowest level. In science, a simple experimental procedure including one or two steps should be coded as Level 1. Other key words that signify a Level 1 include identify, recall,	Level 2 (Skill/Concept) includes the engagement of some mental processing beyond a habitual response. A Level 2 assessment item requires students to make some decisions as to how to approach the problem or activity, whereas Level 1 requires students to demonstrate a rote response, perform a well-known algorithm, follow a set procedure (like a recipe), or perform a clearly defined series of steps. Key words that generally distinguish a Level 2 item include classify, organize, estimate, make observations, collect and display data, and compare data. These actions imply more than one step. For example, to compare data requires first identifying characteristics of the

see next page

Level One	Level Two
recognize, use, and measure. Verbs such as describe and explain could be classified at different levels depending on what is to be described and explained.	objects or phenomenon and then grouping or ordering the objects. Some action verbs, such as explain, describe, or interpret could be classified at different levels depending on the object of the action. For example, if an item required students to explain how light affects mass by indicating there is a relationship between light and heat, this was considered a Level 2. Interpreting information from a simple graph, requiring reading information from the graph, also is a Level 2. Interpreting information from a complex graph that requires some decisions on what features of the graph need to be considered and how information from the graph can be aggregated is a Level 3. Caution is warranted in interpreting Level 2 as only skills because some reviewers will interpret skills very narrowly, as primarily numerical skills, and such interpretation excludes from this level other skills such as visualization skills and probability skills, which may be more complex simply because they are less common. Other Level 2 activities include explaining the purpose and use of experimental procedures; carrying out experimental procedures; making observations and collecting data; classifying, organizing, and comparing data; and organizing and displaying data in tables, graphs, and charts.
Level Three	**Level Four**
Level 3 (Strategic Thinking) requires reasoning, planning, using evidence, and a higher level of thinking than the previous two levels. In most instances, requiring students to explain their thinking is a Level 3. Activities that require students to make conjectures are also at this level. The cognitive demands at Level 3 are complex and abstract. The complexity does not result from the fact that there are multiple answers, a possibility for both Levels 1 and 2, but because the task requires more	Level 4 (Extended Thinking) requires complex reasoning, planning, developing, and thinking most likely over an extended period of time. The extended time period is not a distinguishing factor if the required work is only repetitive and does not require applying significant conceptual understanding and higher-order thinking. For example, if a student has to take the water temperature from a river each day for a month and then construct a graph, this would be classified as a Level 2. However, if the student is to conduct a river study that requires taking into consideration a number of variables, this would be a Level 4. At Level 4, the cognitive demands of the task

see next page

Level Three	Level Four
demanding reasoning. An activity, however, that has more than one possible answer and requires students to justify the response they give would most likely be a Level 3. Other Level 3 activities include drawing conclusions from observations; citing evidence and developing a logical argument for concepts; explaining phenomena in terms of concepts; and using concepts to solve problems.	should be high and the work should be very complex. Students should be required to make several connections—relate ideas *within* the content area or among content areas—and have to select one approach *among* many alternatives on how the situation should be solved, in order to be at this highest level. Level 4 activities include designing and conducting experiments; making connections between a finding and related concepts and phenomena; combining and synthesizing ideas into new concepts; and critiquing experimental designs.

Source: http://facstaff.wcer.wisc.edu/normw/WEBBMonograph%2018AlignmentPaper.pdf

Notice how, with the complexity of descriptions, the levels are truly more than the verbs. For example, in the Level 3 description, Norman Webb notes that: "In most instances, requiring students to explain their thinking is a Level 3. Activities that require students to make conjectures are also at this level. The cognitive demands at Level 3 are complex and abstract. The complexity does not result from the fact that there are multiple answers, a possibility for both Levels 1 and 2, but because the task requires more demanding reasoning."

Considering the depth of the task and/or question is key. It is not enough to simply generate something (a task at the highest level of Bloom's Taxonomy), such as a children's book. A student can complete that task by simply summarizing information. For a DOK Level 3, creation should require analysis of multiple sources, making an argument within that children's book and backing it up with evidence, and critiquing his or her own work to ensure accuracy.

Tool 39
Sample Activities

This may sound a bit overwhelming. Let's look at other possible activities using the DOK's levels. These are samples taken from Webb's Depth of Knowledge Guide Career and Technical Education Definitions.

Sample Activities Based on Webb's DOK

DOK Level	Possible Activities
Level One	Develop a concept map showing a process or describing a topic. Write in your own words. Make a cartoon strip showing the sequence. Paraphrase a chapter. Outline the main points. Basic measurement tasks that involve one step. Use a simple formula where at least one of the unknowns are provided. Locating information in maps, charts, tables, graphs, and drawings.
Level Two	Construct a model to demonstrate how it looks or works. Write a diary/blog entry. Make a topographic map. Write an explanation about this topic for others. Stating relationships among a number of concepts and/or principles. Multi-step calculation tasks. Aggregating/organizing data collected in a basic presentation form.
Level Three	Use a Venn Diagram to compare and contrast. Make a flow chart to show critical stages. Write a letter to the editor after an evaluation product. Prepare a case to present your view about a topic. Explain abstract terms and concepts. Complex calculation problems that draw on multiple processes. Create graphs, tables, and charts where students must reason and organize information with teacher prompts.
Level Four	Applying information to solve ill-defined problems in novel situations. Writing/research tasks that involve formulating and testing hypotheses over time. Perspective taking and collaboration with a group. Creating graphs, tables, and charts where students must reason through and organize information without teacher prompts. Writing tasks with a strong element of persuasion. Write a jingle to advertise a new product.

Samples from www.aps.edu/rda/documents/resources/Webbs_DOK_Guide.pdf

Tool 40
The DOK and Writing

When I was emailing Norman Webb's assistant, he provided another document that I found extremely helpful when looking at the Common Core and other rigorous state standards. His *Depth-of-Knowledge Levels for Four Content Areas* takes four content areas and provides detailed descriptions of what is expected at each level. For our purposes, I chose the writing descriptors, since writing is used across all areas of the curriculum. I'm providing all four levels, but keep in mind rigorous work for most students would be at Levels 3 and 4. Of course, you may have some students developmentally who need to start at Levels 1 and/or 2 and then move forward.

Writing

Level 1

Level 1 requires the student to write or recite simple facts. This writing or recitation does not include complex synthesis or analysis but basic ideas. The students are engaged in listing ideas or words as in a brainstorming activity prior to written composition, are engaged in a simple spelling or vocabulary assessment or are asked to write simple sentences. Students are expected to write and speak using Standard English conventions. This includes using appropriate grammar, punctuation, capitalization, and spelling. Some examples that represent but do not constitute all of Level 1 performance are:

♦ Use punctuation marks correctly.

♦ Identify Standard English grammatical structures and refer to resources for correction.

Level 2

Level 2 requires some mental processing. At this level, students are engaged in first draft writing or brief extemporaneous speaking for a limited number of purposes and audiences. Students are beginning to connect ideas using a simple organizational structure. For example, students may be engaged in note taking, outlining, or simple summaries. Text may be limited to one paragraph. Students demonstrate a basic understanding and appropriate use of such reference materials as a dictionary, thesaurus, or web site. Some examples that represent but do not constitute all of Level 2 performance are:

♦ Construct compound sentences.

♦ Use simple organizational strategies to structure written work.

♦ Write summaries that contain the main idea of the reading selection and pertinent details.

Level 3

Level 3 requires some higher level mental processing. Students are engaged in developing compositions that include multiple paragraphs. These compositions may include complex sentence structure and may demonstrate some synthesis and analysis. Students show awareness of their audience and purpose through focus, organization and the use of appropriate compositional elements. The use of appropriate compositional elements includes such things as addressing chronological order in a narrative or including supporting facts and details in an informational report. At this stage, students are engaged in editing and revising to improve the quality of the composition. Some examples that represent but do not constitute all of Level 3 performance are:

♦ Support ideas with details and examples.

♦ Use voice appropriate to the purpose and audience.

♦ Edit writing to produce a logical progression of ideas.

Level 4

Higher-level thinking is central to Level 4. The standard at this level is a multi-paragraph composition that demonstrates synthesis and analysis of complex ideas or themes. There is evidence of a deep awareness of purpose and audience. For example, informational papers include hypotheses and supporting evidence. Students are expected to create compositions that demonstrate a distinct voice and that stimulate the reader or listener to consider new perspectives on the addressed ideas and themes. An example that represents but does not constitute all of Level 4 performance is:

♦ Write an analysis of two selections, identifying the common theme and generating a purpose that is appropriate for both.

Tool 41
Cognitive Rigor Matrix

Recently, a new tool has emerged: The Cognitive Rigor Matrix. Developed by Karin Hess, Hess' Cognitive Rigor Matrix applies Webb's Depth of Knowledge to Bloom's Taxonomy. Since Bloom focuses of types of thinking needed to complete a task and Webb discusses the depth you need to understand the content to interact with it, the two can work together to provide a comprehensive model for increasing rigor in the classroom.

Hess' Cognitive Rigor Matrix & Curricular Examples: Applying Webb's Depth-of-Knowledge Levels to Bloom's Cognitive Process Dimensions – *Math/Science*

Revised Bloom's Taxonomy	Webb's DOK Level 1 Recall & Reproduction	Webb's DOK Level 2 Skills & Concepts	Webb's DOK Level 3 Strategic Thinking/ Reasoning	Webb's DOK Level 4 Extended Thinking
Remember Retrieve knowledge from long-term memory, recognize, recall, locate, identify	○ Recall, observe, & recognize facts, principles, properties ○ Recall/identify conversions among representations or numbers (e.g., customary and metric measures)			
Understand Construct meaning, clarify, paraphrase, represent, translate, illustrate, give examples, classify, categorize, summarize, generalize, infer a logical conclusion (such as from examples given), predict, compare/contrast, match like ideas, explain, construct models	○ Evaluate an expression ○ Locate points on a grid or number on number line ○ Solve a one-step problem ○ Represent math relationships in words, pictures, or symbols ○ Read, write, compare decimals in scientific notation	○ Specify and explain relationships (e.g., non-examples/examples; cause-effect) ○ Make and record observations ○ Explain steps followed ○ Summarize results or concepts ○ Make basic inferences or logical predictions from data/observations ○ Use models/diagrams to represent or explain mathematical concepts ○ Make and explain estimates	○ Use concepts to solve non-routine problems ○ Explain, generalize, or connect ideas using supporting evidence ○ Make and justify conjectures ○ Explain thinking when more than one response is possible ○ Explain phenomena in terms of concepts	○ Relate mathematical or scientific concepts to other content areas, other domains, or other concepts ○ Develop generalizations of the results obtained and the strategies used (from investigation or readings) and apply them to new problem situations

see next page

Revised Bloom's Taxonomy	Webb's DOK Level 1 Recall & Reproduction	Webb's DOK Level 2 Skills & Concepts	Webb's DOK Level 3 Strategic Thinking/ Reasoning	Webb's DOK Level 4 Extended Thinking
Apply Carry out or use a procedure in a given situation; carry out (apply to a familiar task), or use (apply) to an unfamiliar task	○ Follow simple procedures (recipe-type directions) ○ Calculate, measure, apply a rule (e.g., rounding) ○ Apply algorithm or formula (e.g., area, perimeter) ○ Solve linear equations ○ Make conversions among representations or numbers, or within and between customary and metric measures	○ Select a procedure according to criteria and perform it ○ Solve routine problem applying multiple concepts or decision points ○ Retrieve information from a table, graph, or figure and use it solve a problem requiring multiple steps ○ Translate between tables, graphs, words, and symbolic notations (e.g., graph data from a table) ○ Construct models given criteria	○ Design investigation for a specific purpose or research question ○ Conduct a designed investigation ○ Use concepts to solve non-routine problems ○ Use & show reasoning, planning, and evidence ○ Translate between problem & symbolic notation when not a direct translation	○ Select or devise approach among many alternatives to solve a problem ○ Conduct a project that specifies a problem, identifies solution paths, solves the problem, and reports results
Analyze Break into constituent parts, determine how parts relate, differentiate between relevant-irrelevant, distinguish, focus, select, organize, outline, find coherence, deconstruct	○ Retrieve information from a table or graph to answer a question ○ Identify whether specific information is contained in graphic representations (e.g., table, graph, T-chart, diagram) ○ Identify a pattern/ trend	○ Categorize, classify materials, data, figures based on characteristics ○ Organize or order data ○ Compare/contrast figures or data ○ Select appropriate graph and organize & display data ○ Interpret data from a simple graph ○ Extend a pattern	○ Compare information within or across data sets or texts ○ Analyze and draw conclusions from data, citing evidence ○ Generalize a pattern ○ Interpret data from complex graph ○ Analyze similarities/ differences between procedures or solutions	○ Analyze multiple sources of evidence ○ Analyze complex/ abstract themes ○ Gather, analyze, and evaluate information

see next page

Revised Bloom's Taxonomy	Webb's DOK Level 1 Recall & Reproduction	Webb's DOK Level 2 Skills & Concepts	Webb's DOK Level 3 Strategic Thinking/ Reasoning	Webb's DOK Level 4 Extended Thinking
Evaluate Make judgments based on criteria, check, detect inconsistencies or fallacies, judge, critique			○ Cite evidence and develop a logical argument for concepts or solutions ○ Describe, compare, and contrast solution methods ○ Verify reasonableness of results	○ Gather, analyze, & evaluate information to draw conclusions ○ Apply understanding in a novel way, provide argument or justification for the application
Create Reorganize elements into new patterns/structures, generate, hypothesize, design, plan, construct, produce	○ Brainstorm ideas, concepts, or perspectives related to a topic	○ Generate conjectures or hypotheses based on observations or prior knowledge and experience	○ Synthesize information within one dataset, source, or text ○ Formulate an original problem given a situation ○ Develop a scientific/ mathematical model for a complex situation	○ Synthesize information across multiple sources or texts ○ Design a mathematical model to inform and solve a practical or abstract situation

Hess' Cognitive Rigor Matrix & Curricular Examples: Applying Webb's Depth-of-Knowledge Levels to Bloom's Cognitive Process Dimensions – *ELA*

Revised Bloom's Taxonomy	Webb's DOK Level 1 Recall & Reproduction	Webb's DOK Level 2 Skills & Concepts	Webb's DOK Level 3 Strategic Thinking/ Reasoning	Webb's DOK Level 4 Extended Thinking
Remember Retrieve knowledge from long-term memory, recognize, recall, locate, identify	○ Recall, recognize, or locate basic facts, details, events, or ideas explicit in texts ○ Read words orally in connected text with fluency & accuracy			
Understand Construct meaning, clarify, paraphrase, represent, translate, illustrate, give examples, classify, categorize, summarize, generalize, infer a logical conclusion, predict, compare/contrast, match like ideas, explain, construct models	○ Identify or describe literary elements (characters, setting, sequence, etc.) ○ Select appropriate words when intended meaning/definition is clearly evident ○ Describe/explain who, what, where, when, or how ○ Define/describe facts, details, terms, principles ○ Write simple sentences	○ Specify, explain, show relationships; explain why, cause-effect ○ Give non-examples/examples ○ Summarize results, concepts, ideas ○ Make basic inferences of logical predictions from data or texts ○ Identify main ideas or accurate generalizations of texts ○ Locate information to support explicit-implicit central ideas	○ Explain, generalize, or connect ideas using supporting evidence (quote, example, text reference) ○ Identify/make inferences about explicit or implicit themes ○ Describe how word choice, point of view, or bias may affect the readers' interpretation of a text ○ Write multi-paragraph composition for specific purpose, focus, voice, tone, & audience	○ Explain how concepts or ideas specifically relate to *other* content domains or concepts ○ Develop generalizations of the results obtained or strategies used and apply them to new problem situations

see next page

see next page

Revised Bloom's Taxonomy	Webb's DOK Level 1 Recall & Reproduction	Webb's DOK Level 2 Skills & Concepts	Webb's DOK Level 3 Strategic Thinking/ Reasoning	Webb's DOK Level 4 Extended Thinking
Apply Carry out or use a procedure in a given situation; carry out (apply to a familiar task), or use (apply) to an unfamiliar task	○ Use language structure (pre/suffix) or word relationships (synonym/antonym) to determine meaning of words ○ Apply rules of resources to edit spelling, grammar, punctuation, conventions, word use ○ Apply basic formats for documenting sources	○ Use context to identify the meaning of words/phrases ○ Obtain and interpret information using text features ○ Develop a text that may be limited to one paragraph ○ Apply simple organizational structures (paragraph, sentence types) in writing	○ Apply a concept in a new context ○ Revise final draft for meaning or progression of ideas ○ Apply internal consistency of text organization and structure to composing a full composition ○ Apply word choice, point of view, style to impact readers'/viewers' interpretation of a text	○ Illustrate how multiple themes (historical, geographic, social) may be interrelated ○ Select or devise an approach among many alternatives to research a novel problem
Analyze Break into constituent parts, determine how parts relate, differentiate between relevant-irrelevant, distinguish, focus, select, organize, outline, find coherence, deconstruct (e.g., for bias or point of view)	○ Identify whether specific information is contained in graphic representations (e.g., map, chart, table, graph, T-chart, diagram) or text features (e.g., headings, subheadings, captions) ○ Decide which text structure is appropriate to audience and purpose	○ Categorize/compare literary elements, terms, facts/details, events ○ Identify use of literary devices ○ Analyze format, organization, & internal text structure (signal words, transitions, semantic cues) of different texts ○ Distinguish: relevant-irrelevant information; fact/opinion ○ Identify characteristic text features; distinguish between texts, genres	○ Analyze information within data sets or texts ○ Analyze interrelationships among concepts, issues, problems ○ Analyze or interpret author's craft (literacy devices, viewpoint, or potential bias) to create or critique a text ○ Use reasoning, planning, and evidence to support inferences	○ Analyze multiple sources of evidence, or multiple works by the same author, or across genres, time periods, themes ○ Analyze complex/abstract themes, perspectives, concepts ○ Gather, analyze, and organize multiple information sources ○ Analyze discourse styles

Revised Bloom's Taxonomy	Webb's DOK Level 1 Recall & Reproduction	Webb's DOK Level 2 Skills & Concepts	Webb's DOK Level 3 Strategic Thinking/ Reasoning	Webb's DOK Level 4 Extended Thinking
Evaluate Make judgments based on criteria, check, detect inconsistencies or fallacies, judge, critique			○ Cite evidence and develop a logical argument for conjectures ○ Describe, compare, and contrast solution methods ○ Verify reasonableness of results ○ Justify or critique conclusions drawn	○ Evaluate relevancy, accuracy, & completeness of information from multiple sources ○ Apply understanding in a novel way, provide argument or justification for the application
Create Reorganize elements into new patterns/structures, generate, hypothesize, design, plan, produce	○ Brainstorm ideas, concepts, or perspectives related to a topic or concept	○ Generate conjectures or hypotheses based on observations or prior knowledge and experience	○ Synthesize information within one source or text ○ Develop a complex model for a given situation ○ Develop an alternative solution	○ Synthesize information across multiple sources or texts ○ Articulate a new voice, alternate theme, new knowledge or perspective

© 2009 Karin K. Hess: Hess' Cognitice Rigor Matrix: Permission to reproduce is given when authorship is fully cited [khess@nciea.org]

For full article, go to www.nciea.org

Tool 42
Costa's House of Questions

Costa and Kallick (2008), authors of *Learning and Leading with Habits of Mind*, provide a different model. It is a three-level, user-friendly, practical story house that describes the levels of questioning. I've observed this model used in several AVID (Advancement Via Individual Determination, www.avid .org) classrooms, and it is effective for both students and teachers.

Costa's House of Questioning

Level	Verbs
Level One (lowest)—gather information	Complete, identify, recite, define, list, select, describe, observe.
Level Two (middle)—process information	Compare, contrast, classify, sort, distinguish, explain, infer, analyze.
Level three (highest)—apply information	Evaluate, generalize, imagine, judge, predict, speculate, if/then, hypothesize, forecast.

Tool 43
Samples for Costa's House of Questions

Let's look at how Costa's House of Questions can be applied in math, reading, and science.

Applying Costa's Questions

Math	Reading
Level One: Define array Level Two: Compare and contrast an array to an area grid. Level Three: Make an array into a word problem.	Level One: Describe how the Big Bad Wolf destroyed the pigs' houses. Level Two: Compare and contrast the Three Little Pigs and the True Story of the Three Little Pigs Level Three: Judge what you believe is the true character of the Big Bad World and provide evidence to support your position.
Science	
Level One: Describe the approach you took to solve the problem. Level Two: Explain and sequence the steps of the science experiment used to arrive at solution. Level Three: Hypothesize the outcome of the science experiment.	

Tool 44
The QUILT Model of Questioning

The QUILT model of questioning was developed and tested in the Appalachian Educational Laboratory in the 1990s. The program, which included intensive staff development, promoted intensive teacher understanding of questioning skills, which would then result in an increase in students' thinking levels. There are five stages to the questioning process.

Five Stages of the QUILT Model

Stage 1: Prepare the question
- Identify instructional purpose.
- Determine content focus.
- Select cognitive level.
- Consider wording and syntax.

Stage 2: Present the question
- Indicate response format.
- Ask the question.
- Select respondent.

Stage 3: Prompt student responses
- Pause after asking question.
- Assist nonrespondent.
- Pause following student response.

Stage 4: Process student responses
- Provide appropriate feedback.
- Expand and use correct responses.
- Elicit student reactions and questions.

Stage 5: Critique the questioning episode
- Analyze the questions.
- Map respondent selection.
- Evaluate student response patterns.
- Examine teacher and student reactions.

Source: www2.ed.gov/pubs/triedandtrue/quest.html

Tool 45
Marzano's Five Dimensions of Thinking

In 1988, Marzano and his colleagues released a framework called the Five Dimensions of Thinking. It was designed to provide a way to look at different techniques of thinking.

Five Dimensions of Thinking

Dimension	Explanation
Metacognition	Awareness and Control of Thinking
Critical and Creative Thinking	Critical: Analyzing and Assessing Evidence and/or Reasoning Creative: Applying Strategies
Thinking Processes	Multi-step Thinking Skills Such as Problem-Solving, Research, and Decision-Making
Core Thinking Skills	Infer, Analyze, Compare, Summarize, Verify
Connecting Thinking to Content Knowledge	Apply to Specific Content Areas

As you can see from the chart, these thinking skills are very similar to those in other models, they are just framed differently. One key difference is that Marzano and his co-authors specifically address being aware of and controlling one's thinking (metacognition).

Tool 46
Essential Questions

Another way to look at questioning is through the seven defining characteristics of essential questions. As McTighe and Wiggins (2013) explain, the "aim is to stimulate thought, to provoke inquiry, and to spark more questions including thoughtful student questions, not just page answers. They are provocative and generative. By tackling such questions, learners are engaged in uncovering the depth and richness of a topic that might otherwise be obscured by simply covering it" (p. 3).

Seven Defining Characteristics of Essential Questions
1. It is open ended.
2. It is thought-provoking and intellectually engaging.
3. Calls for higher-order thinking.

4. Points toward important, transferable ideas.

5. Raises additional questions.

6. Requires support and justification.

7. Recurs over time.

Let's look at a sample of their questioning framework in a lesson revolving around the September 11 attack on the United States.

Applying the McTighe and Wiggins Framework

Facet	Sample Question
Explanation	What are causes and effects of the 9/11 attack?
Interpretation	Why do they hate us or is hate the right term?
Application	What might prevent another 9/11 or can we?
Perspective	What is the jihadists' story of 9/11?
Empathy	What motivates a suicide bomber?
Self-Knowledge	In what ways did 9/11 change me or my life?

Tool 47
Ciardello's Four Levels of Questions

In "Did you ask a good question today?", Angelo V. Ciardello (1998) identified four types of questions, as well as corresponding question stems and cognitive operations. They are simple, but provide a clear framework for crafting questions and assignments.

Ciardello's Four Levels of Questions

Types of Questions	Cognitive Operations	Prompts
Memory	Encourage naming, defining, identifying, designating, or answering yes/no	list, define, tell, describe, identify, show, label, collect, examine, tabulate, quote, name, who, when, where
Convergent	Encourage explaining, stating relationships, comparing, and contrasting	combine, integrate, modify, rearrange, substitute, plan, create, design, invent, what if?, compose, formulate, prepare, generalize, rewrite
Divergent	Encourage predicting, hypothesizing, inferring, reconstructing	summarize, describe, interpret, contrast, predict, associate, distinguish, estimate, differentiate, discuss, extend

see next page

Types of Questions	Cognitive Operations	Prompts
Evaluative	Encourage valuing, judging, defending, justifying choices	assess, decide, rank, grade, test, measure, recommend, convince, select, judge, explain, discriminate, support, conclude, compare, summarize

Tool 48
Socratic Questioning

When I was teaching, I learned about the Paideia Seminar. A critical part of the seminar discussions was the notion of Socratic Questioning. Although some questions were provided for guidance, I still struggled with asking questions at the highest levels. In 2006, Richard Paul expanded his earlier list of six types of Socratic Questions to nine categories. They are useful as you help students develop metacognition, or the concept of thinking about their own thinking.

Questions for a Socratic Dialogue

Types of Question	Samples
Questions of Clarification	What do you mean by _____? What is your main point? Could you give me an example?
Questions that Probe Purpose	What was your purpose when you said _____? How do the purposes of these two groups vary? Was this purpose justifiable?
Questions that Probe Assumptions	What are you assuming? All of your reasoning depends on the idea that _____. Why have you based your reasoning on xxx rather than _____? Why do you think the assumption holds here?
Questions that Probe Information, Reasoning, Evidence, and Causes	What are your reasons for saying that? What led you to that belief? How could we go about finding out whether that is true?
Questions About Viewpoints or Perspectives	You seem to be approaching this issue from xxx perspective. Why have you chosen this perspective rather than that perspective? Can/did anyone see this another way?
Questions that Probe Implications and Consequences	What are you implying by that? Would that necessarily happen or only probably happen? If this and this are the case, then what else must be true?

see next page

Types of Question	Samples
Questions About the Question	How could someone settle this question? Can we break this question down at all? Why is this question important?
Questions that Probe Concepts	Do these two ideas conflict? If so, how? How is this idea guiding our thinking as we try to reason through this issue? Is this idea causing us problems? Which main distinctions should we draw in reasoning through this problem?
Questions that Probe Inferences and Interpretations	What information are we basing this conclusion? Is there a more logical inference we might make in this situation? Given all the facts, what is the best possible conclusion?

Tool 49
Effective Questions

Finally, I've developed a list of nine characteristics of effective questioning, using the acrostic for QUESTIONS.

> **Q**uality Triumphs over Quantity
> **U**nderestimate—Don't
> **E**ncourage Other Questions
> **S**tudent-Ownership Created
> **T**urn Attention to Deeper Issues
> **I**gnite Other Questions
> **O**nward and Upward
> **N**uanced, Not Simplistic
> **S**how Relationships

Quality Triumphs over Quantity

As you develop questions, remember that quality is more important that quantity. Sometimes, it's easy to get focused on the sheer quantity of information to be covered, and we pepper students with questions. For effective questioning, choose fewer questions with more depth.

Underestimate—Don't

Don't underestimate your students' abilities to think at higher levels. I know when I first started teaching, because my students were reluctant to answer questions, I assumed I needed to make them easier. What I later realized was that my students simply needed more encouragement, especially since they were reluctant to answer the easier questions too! It wasn't the level of the questioning; it was that they didn't want to be embarrassed in front of their peers if they missed the answer.

Encourage Other Questions

The best questions encourage other questions from students. Ideally, when you ask a question and a student answers it, other students are prompted to ask questions such as, "Why do you think that?" or "What else happens?" At times, your questions will also encourage other questions from you—ones that facilitate understanding and that point out something pertinent from the text or resource.

Student-Ownership Created

You also want to create student ownership. When students take control of the discussion, staying on point, and becoming truly involved in the conversation, you see high levels of student engagement. If students feel like the discussion is theirs, rather than yours, you've created an environment in which students can thrive.

Turn Attention to Deeper Issues

Effective questioning also occurs when you turn your attention to deeper issues, rather than staying at a surface level. I know when I was teaching, there were times I felt tremendous pressure just to keep up the pace of the material. Occasionally, it felt as though I was covering the material, but not really teaching it. We need to make sure we dig into the content with our students, probing them to think about the deeper meaning of the material.

Ignite Other Questions

In addition to just encouraging other questions, you want to ignite other questions. Think about it—rather than simply encouraging students to think of their own questions, you also want to teach them to initiate questioning without any prompting from you. It's like lighting a flame of a candle—once it's lit, you don't need to do anything else. You've probably led a discussion like that, where the students truly take over the conversation and you become, to some degree, an observer. This doesn't mean students are off-topic; rather, they are totally immersed in the content.

Onward and Upward

I was recently asked, "Is there a place for lower-level questions in a classroom?" The answer is yes. At times, we need to start with a more basic, informational question so that we can move onward and upward to the higher levels. We must never forget that higher-level questions require a student to know basic information and then apply it for analysis and reflection.

Nuanced, Not Simplistic

Effective questions should be understandable by students, but that doesn't mean they have to be simplistic. They can be nuanced, requiring students to think not only about the answer, but also about the question. We want students to think about their own thinking, and nuanced questioning encourages it.

Show Relationships

Finally, effective questions should show relationships among different concepts, subject areas, or the student and real life. We would prefer that students see these relationships themselves, but they often do not. Therefore, our questions can guide them to making connections.

Tool 50
Students' Responses to Questions

Although we've dealt extensively with questioning, high expectations are more than just the questions we ask; we also must consider the answers we accept from students. For example, I regularly visit classrooms where the teachers are asking great high-level questions, but they are also accepting one word, low-level responses. When I was a teacher, I was so grateful to get an answer, I just moved on to the next student. But when students don't respond at an equally high level, we need to ask probing or extending questions, such as "Will you explain that a little more?", "How did you know that answer?", or "That's a good start; can you give me more detail?"

What we don't want to do is simply accept a basic answer and then just move on to another student. This sends a message that we know that they can't give us a better answer. Granted, the student may need support and guiding questions to help them answer at a more in-depth level. But we still need to help them get there.

Adult Behaviors

In *The Art and Science of Teaching* (2007) Robert Marzano describes actions by teachers that are representative of lowered expectations. There are multiple examples in research of the different acts that are reflective of both high and low expectations. There are three specific adult behaviors that can increase expectations in your classroom.

Tool 51
Attention

First, our attention matters. For some students, especially those who are quiet and well mannered, we simply don't give them any extra attention. After all, we're busy with those who demand our attention. But by leaving out these "middle of the road" students, we are not pushing them to higher levels of learning. Then there are those who demand our attention in negative ways. These are the students who are more often at-risk, and who tend to be labeled as discipline problems. They may have behavior issues, but these are also the students who are constantly asking questions, sometimes the same question over and over again. We may give them the immediate attention they require, but then we move on. Finally, there are those students who are models in the classroom. They are positively engaged in learning, volunteer to participate, do their homework, and are generally considered ideal students. They tend to receive the most positive attention from us.

What is important to consider is that under this model, which happens far more often than we'd like to admit, not all students receive the appropriate amount of positive attention focused on learning. We must be sure to attend to the learning of our students, and tailor that attention to their specific needs. At times this may be difficult due to behavioral issues, but we do need to deal with the behavior in ways to allow us to focus on learning. But that's a topic for another book!

Tool 52
Wait Time and Opportunities to Answer

Another adult behavior that makes a difference is how we deal with questioning of our students. For example, with students at-risk, we are more likely to give them less wait time. We also tend to call on them less often, in part because we haven't necessarily received positive answers in the past. Again, though, this evidences low expectations—it sends the message that we don't think they can, so we don't call on them or give them appropriate time to answer. Providing adequate wait time and opportunities for all students to respond are critical behaviors we should exhibit.

Tool 53
Feedback and Follow-Up

Finally, we can make a difference in the ways we provide feedback and follow-up with students. In order to demonstrate high expectations, we should provide appropriate, positive feedback and follow-up when a student is learning. Often, this does not happen with students for whom we have low expectations. In those cases, we tend to provide general, rather than specific feedback, and little to no follow-up. In contrast, when we have high expectations for students, we provide specific feedback for growth, and we follow-up with the student on a regular basis to ensure progress. When we find ourselves exhibiting low-expectation behaviors, we need to switch gears in order to ensure we are expecting each of our students can and will learn at high levels.

Expecting the Best

When I taught students who were at risk, it was difficult to see their potential. Although I'm a big believer in viewing students as "butterflies-in-the-making," there were days that my students seemed to be wrapped up in a chrysalis, or slowly crawling along like caterpillars. They certainly didn't seem to be beautiful butterflies! One of the most difficult things for teachers to do is to keep our expectations high, especially when our students' actions make us think less of them. There were days my students challenged me to come up with any positive thoughts about them, but those were the days they needed me the most. I found they needed me to believe they are butterflies when they are most acting like worms! I found that it's particularly during those times they need us to give them our BEST.

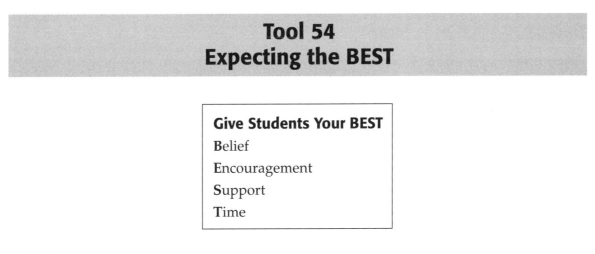

Belief

The most basic characteristic to invest in your students is a strong belief that they are important, valued, and capable. If you believe in your students, you will call on each one to give them an opportunity to share a response. You'll also stick with them when they don't know an answer. For example, if La'Quandra doesn't know, or stumbles with an answer, I have several possible responses. I can tell her she is wrong, call on another student to help her out, answer for her, or give up and move on to another question. However, another alternative is to use a series of questions to guide her to the correct answer. I might go to another student for help, but I continue to come back to Michelle until she demonstrates understanding. By doing so, I show her that I believe she can learn.

Encouragement

Students who do not have a lot of self-confidence need a steady stream of encouragement. Encouragement is communicated through appropriate praise and feedback, as well as nonverbal cues such as a smile. Encouragement is always a signal to the student to keep trying. It's important to encourage students regularly, especially when they are less successful. Think back to the example we just discussed. When a student is struggling to answer a question, it's important to encourage them with supportive comments while guiding them to the correct answer. Focus on their strengths to give them the confidence to continue.

Support

Providing support to accompany increased expectations is not an option. This can be as basic as guiding students through responses as in the prior example. However, it also includes ensuring that each student has access to the resources needed to accomplish more rigorous tasks. Finally, as teachers, we need to build scaffolding into projects and assignments so that students can be successful. We'll focus on that in Chapter Five: Give Support.

Time

Ultimately, inspiring students through your belief, encouragement, and support requires that you make a choice to invest your time in particular students. This is evidenced in two specific ways. First, it is critical to allow appropriate wait time for every student to answer. Some students need more time to reflect before they are ready to respond. That's one of the reasons I like the strategy of Think-Pair-Share. After you ask a question, ask everyone to stop and think for approximately 45 seconds to a minute. It allows students to have more time to reflect before you ask for a group answer.

You may also choose to pay extra attention to those students who are sometimes overlooked. In fewer than five minutes per day, you can say an extra positive comment several times during the day. Or, you can write additional feedback on a student's paper or schedule time to meet with a student during the school day to go over material he or she doesn't understand. The important part is not the amount of time you spend; it is that you commit to doing these things consistently with the students who need you.

Learning is Not Optional

Another aspect of high expectations is communicating that learning is not optional. Many students think it's okay to "take a zero," and in a rigorous classroom, that is not acceptable.

Tool 55
Refuse to Use the Word "W

I took several teachers and the principal from a local school to v.
school in a neighboring state. The school had a strong reputation for closi.̪ɡ
ment gaps, despite the challenging student population. Bob Heath, the principa.̪ ˍ
local middle school, describes his experience:

The option to not do work was not there. If as adults, we accept that students cannot do work,
we are not doing the kids any service at all. This comes out in several ways, starting with
our vocabulary. If we say "Students just won't do the work," we are part of the problem. We
have to get those words out of our vocabulary. They won't do because we don't make them do.

Don't Allow "Won't"

Tool 56
Don't Allow the Word "Can't"

When I was teaching, my students' default response to assignments was, "I can't do
that." It became so automatic to them, that they would answer "I can't" before I asked
them to do something. Finally, I added it to our classroom rules: You are not allowed
to use the word can't. It took about six weeks, but students stopped using the word. I
was in an elementary school in Cleveland, Ohio, and a teacher shared her response to
the same issue. Each student took a can, and filled it with sheets of paper noting all the
things they couldn't do. Then, they buried their "can'ts" and started fresh.

Don't Allow "Can't"

Tool 57
Each Student Demonstrates Understanding

Another way to show students that learning is not optional is to require each student to demonstrate he or she understands your content throughout the lesson. For example, when we call on one student, we have allowed all the other students to disengage. We assume they also know the answer, and if we ask students if they agree with the student who responded, the others tend to nod. But that doesn't really mean they understand. Instead, look for options such as pair-share that require each student to respond individually, with a partner, or in a small group so that they truly demonstrate understanding of the content.

Strategies for Involving Each Student

Thumbs Up and Thumbs Down

Computer Response Clickers

Individual Whiteboards

iPad Interactive Whiteboards (such as ShowMe)

Reciprocal Teaching

Jigsaw Cooperative Learning Groups

Tool 58
Required Completion of Work

If something is important enough for you to assign it, then it should be important enough for a student to complete it. Let me clarify a key point. This is not just about the student's responsibility. You play a major role in his or her success. First, it means we design assignments that are valuable, not just busy work. In addition to helping students understand the value of the work, we hold them responsible for completion.

When I was teaching, that meant that students who did not complete an assignment stayed with me during lunch and completed it while eating. You don't have to give up your lunchtime, but requiring students to complete something means you also provide a structure and support to ensure they finish. I was recently in a high school where the teachers posted office hours for students to receive extra help. That's a great idea, but the students who need the most help usually don't voluntarily seek it. Another school in the same district offered specified times for help, but it was required for any student who failed a test. The teachers sent a clear message that learning was not a choice. You'll find more information on this in Chapter Five, Tool 125.

Conclusion

Raising your expectations of students is foundational to increasing rigor in your classroom. Increasing our levels of questioning, adjusting our adult behaviors, and insisting that learning is not optional are concrete ways we can exhibit high expectations.

Reflection into Action

1. What are three main tools from this chapter you could use in your classroom?

2. Which of those three will you put into place in the next three days?

3. Are there any resources you need to make this happen?

4. Which one would you like to implement next week?

5. What other tools do you want to consider for the future?

6. Is there anything else from this chapter you want to remember after you finish the book?

4
Increase Depth of Instruction

In this chapter, we'll look at options to increase the depth of your instruction. What you'll notice throughout the activities is a shift to student ownership of learning, as well as the need to think at higher levels to complete the activities. There is a particular focus on students' reflecting on their own learning. Although you will encounter technology throughout the chapter, I have tried to steer away from too many specific websites, since they change so quickly.

Lesson Starters
Literacy Across the Curriculum
Working with Other Students
Real-Life Learning Applications
Opportunities for Review

Lesson Starters

A critical part of every lesson is the starting point. Without a strong kick-off to the lesson, prior knowledge may not be activated, and learning may not be focused. Let's look at several tools for introducing a lesson.

Tool 59
Deductive vs. Inductive Reasoning

One decision to make as you begin a lesson is whether you would like students to use deductive or inductive reasoning. In deductive learning, students are given a standard, topic, or concept at the start of the class, and the lesson about it follows. In inductive learning, students are given examples of the topic or concept and, through the lesson, they are guided to learn the concept. Both methods are appropriate and require students to think at higher levels.

Deductive vs. Inductive Reasoning

Deductive Reasoning	Inductive Reasoning
Top Down (state learning objective first)	Bottom Up (students generate the specified objective from examples)

Tool 60
Beginning with Authentic Learning

We often talk about the importance of real-life learning in the classroom. However, many times we have students complete application activities at the end of a lesson. In a rigorous classroom, we can flip this to apply the inductive model. Jessica Guidry, one of my former students, designed an ecology unit for her science classroom that applies this principle. Her students were introduced to the unit with the following task:

> *You are an ecologist from Rock Hill, South Carolina. Recently, members of the United Nations have come together and decided that they must eliminate one biome to make room for the world's growing human population. You and a group of your peers have decided to take a stand. You will each choose one biome to present to the United Nations in New York City this April. It is very important that you persuade the members of the UN to keep your chosen biome alive! The UN has asked that you write a persuasive essay to present to the audience. They also asked that you bring visuals and information about your references. You must be sure that you include how your biome benefits the world population. You need to include information about the habitats, populations, animals, plants, and food chains of your biome.*

Throughout the unit, she integrated a variety of other open-ended projects, such as creating a flip book on their biome, participating in a debate, and creating food chains/webs in addition to the regular mix of lecture, guided discussion, and laboratory activities. However, since she began with the open-ended, authentic situation, her students were more engaged and challenged throughout the lessons.

Tool 61
Standards

Many teachers write the standard for the day on the board. Students are then expected to either read the standard, write the standard, or the teacher reads the standard aloud. Too often, this becomes a rote activity that carries no real meaning for students. In order to activate learning, turn the statement into a question. Explain to students that the focus of the day is for them to be able to answer the question at the end of the lesson. Then, as a final activity for the day, ask them to write the answer and turn it in.

Tool 62
Uncovering Pictures

Building on the notion of inductive teaching, while introducing a concept or topic for the day, use a picture. Rather than showing the entire picture to students, cut the picture into multiple pieces, and show them one at a time, requiring them to discern elements and infer the topic. You can also use technology to either show pieces or uncover pieces of the picture. I was in a primary classroom where the teacher used a simple folder to complete this activity. On the front of the folder, a face with a smile was cut out. The picture was inserted inside the folder, and students determined the picture with just the portion seen through the face. It's a simple way to complete this activity.

Tool 63
Discover the Mistakes

For the topic you will be teaching today, create a webpage or blog entry that mimics an online encyclopedia entry. Include at least four content errors. Ask students to compare the webpage to a credible site, such as the National Geographic Channel. Their task is to correct the mistakes. This is a great way to build some prior knowledge and hone students' analysis skills.

Tool 64
Word Sorts

Word Sorts is a simple game with increased complexity. Give students a variety of words or concepts that can be categorized. You might use two categories for comparison and contrast, or three or more for more complex analysis. Students work in small groups to sort the words into the determined number of categories. Their completed word sorts are then used to springboard a discussion of the concepts.

Tool 65
Entrance Slips

Entrance slips can be used in a variety of ways. First, you can hand students a post-it note or index card as they enter the room or start a lesson. Ask them to write down one thing they learned from yesterday's lesson, and one question they have. Take these up and use them as a lesson kickoff or a discussion starter. Another option is to simply give students three to five minutes at the beginning of class to write down what they learned from the prior day's lesson and any homework. Students can then share from their reflections in a class discussion.

Literacy Across the Curriculum

Literacy, which includes reading, writing, listening, and speaking, is critical to all areas of the curriculum. One common refrain is that English/Language Arts teachers should teach these subjects. However, teachers of science, social studies, math, the arts, and career and technology must address these areas in order to help students unlock their content. Students must use literacy in all areas in order to prepare for 21st-century living. Finally, the Common Core requires literacy to be applied in all areas. It is so important that there are separate literacy standards at grades 6–12. Incorporating literacy in all subject areas is not difficult. There are strategies that can be used across all areas of the curriculum.

Tool 66
Storyboards

I find it effective to teach sequencing of events or a process through Storyboarding. In a science classroom, I ask students to brainstorm ideas of different steps that might occur during an experiment, either drawing or writing each idea on a separate sticky note. They can reorder their steps based on what actually works during the experiment, adding in any steps they may have left out.

In writing, students can plan an essay or research paper using this process. After they write their ideas and research, students can order and reorder the ideas by rearranging the sticky notes. You can also simply use a template (below). I explained to my students that this is a simple version of storyboarding, which is how Walt Disney planned his movies.

Sample Template for Storyboarding

Tool 67
Technology and Storyboarding

You can also use a variety of technology sources for storyboarding. For example, sites such as www.timeline.com and www.linoit.com allow students to create their own storyboards electronically. Another option is to have students choose from a set of photos online (be sure to screen the photos in advance) to use as a basis for their storyboard. There are also some programs that will allow students to organize their photos and record their story via audio.

Tool 68
Newspapers

Chris Triolo encouraged his students to develop an understanding of science concepts through the creation of a newspaper. As he explains in the assignment:

> *You are the editor of* Plant Daily News *(or some newspaper of your choice). Your task is to design the front page of today's newspaper. As with a newspaper, the front page should be divided into sections. You should have each of the eight concepts we have learned in one or more of the sections. You must receive a score of 8–10 in order to have your article featured on the cover page. Be sure to follow the editor's suggestions.*

This could easily be adapted to create a website, which would encourage even more engagement from today's tech-savvy learners.

Tool 69
Blogs and Wikis

Blogs, short (less than 350 word) entries, allow students to create a series of extended responses on a particular topic. For example, after students read a story or novel, they can write their response to the text. Many teachers use wikis, which is a way to power your blogs and allow for students to write back and forth.

A key aspect of blogs is the written response by others, which requires the blog author to expand on the original response. Dave Craig used a blog with his fifth graders for reader response. After their initial entry about their book, other students responded with additional questions. The back-and-forth necessitates that the original author write at higher levels. As you begin, you may want to assign students particular blogs to write a response with questions.

Sample Blog Assignment

Choose a person who is famous (related to our subject area). Create a blog entry explaining who you are and why you are famous. You can expect a minimum of five follow-up questions from other students and/or the teacher. Be prepared to answer them with additional information about your person.

Tool 70
Video Reporting

One of my son's favorite activities is recording his friends skateboarding and editing the clips. He used these techniques in one of his match classes to analyze the math skills used in skateboarding. Given a choice of assignments, he would rather create a video than write a paper.

Students can create a video report on a wide range of topics in almost any class. Simply start with a topic, ask students to choose a perspective, and start filming. I've seen this used for students to create character profiles, job descriptions, and mini-talk shows. It's an engaging, motivating activity. However, as with all activities, provide structure and guidelines to ensure students move beyond a basic assignment to one that requires higher levels of thinking.

Sample Video Reporting Activities

Interview with a Historical Figure
News Report of a Current or Past Event
Profile of Math Applications of a Sport
Demonstration of the Water Cycle
Model Job Interview

Tool 71
Thought or Speech Bubbles

One alternative for helping students think about thinking is through the use of thought bubbles. As they plan their writing, they use bubbles to describe what different characters are thinking. Then, when they write a first draft, it's easier to include the thoughts of each character because they have specifically planned for that. You can also use thought bubbles to describe the thoughts for each side of an issue or debate.

Another option is to use speech bubbles. There are several ways to utilize speech bubbles. First, in a career class, students can create a storyboard with a conversation between an employer and employee. Next, if researching a historical figure or scientist, ask your class to create a timeline of speech bubbles of comments from the person. Finally, in a language arts/English class, speech bubbles are a great way to revisit the characters from a story or a novel. Another student-friendly adaptation is to use text messages rather than speech bubbles.

Tool 72
Propaganda

Students often are unable to distinguish between fact, opinion, and propaganda. As one of my students commented, "Isn't everything I see true?" Particularly as students gather more and more information from the internet, it's important to help them understand propaganda.

One of the lessons that surprised my students was on advertising. I showed them a range of ads about various products, and we discussed what they saw. Their initial responses revolved around how pretty, handsome, successful, and happy the people appeared to be. That led to a discussion of advertising techniques and propaganda. Students quickly realized that it's important to look beneath the surface to determine the real meaning of ads.

I was recently in Lynn Kelley's classroom, where she did a similar activity. After teaching types of propaganda, her students created videos demonstrating the various techniques. Another alternative is to ask students to interpret editorial cartoons, and determine whether the cartoons use propaganda techniques to communicate a message.

Tool 73
Cubing

Cubing allows students to look at a topic or issue from six perspectives. At a basic level, the sides of the cube are labeled who, what, when, where, why, and how. Students would then write about or answer the questions for each side of the block.

Story Cubing Pattern

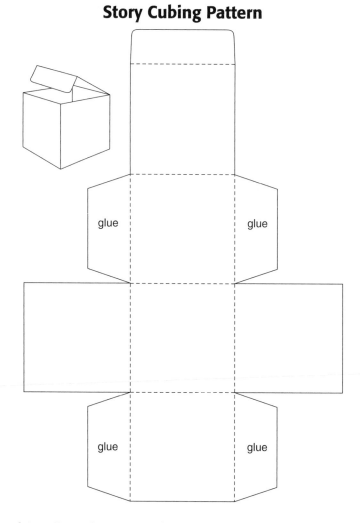

When I was teaching, I used more sophisticated prompts for writing. They required my students to move beyond a basic answer to more complex responses.

Cubing Prompts

Describe It (the topic or issue)

Compare It

Associate It

Analyze It

Apply It

Argue For or Against It

One of the benefits of cubing is that you can use a variety of prompts, depending on your specific grade level and/or subject area. A caution, however; be sure your prompts are appropriate for the topic and encourage higher level thinking, rather than just being a cute worksheet.

Other Possible Cubing Prompts

Define It

Explain It

Locate It

Solve It

Illustrate It

Diagram It

Research It

Write a Sentence (or Paragraph) with It

A final way to use cubes is to write different assignments on each side of the cube. Students can "roll the cube" physically or electronically to determine their activity, or you can assign specific sides to them. It's a great option for differentiating instruction.

Tool 74
Decision Chart

Decision Charts are another way for students to view an issue from a variety of perspectives. Following the template below, students write the issue. Next, they write

Decision Tree Template

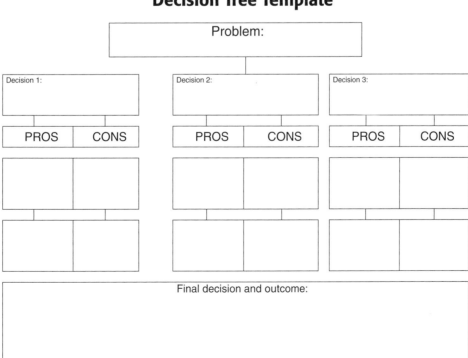

the different options that could occur in response to the issue. Finally, they write the pros and cons of each response. The charts can then be used as a starting point for a class or small group discussion, an essay or extended response, or a debate.

Tool 75
Text Connections

Every time you introduce a new concept or text to students, whether it is a book, article, or even a word, it's important to connect it to other texts they have read or other information they have learned. I was in a classroom where the teacher had a huge bulletin board at the front of the room. Students had drawn book covers for all books and other texts they had read. Whenever the class read a new book, the teacher posted a cover, and students used string to connect the new book with any other books that were related. The class created a visual web of connections for everyone to see.

In my social studies class, I found I needed to encourage my students to think deeper about those connections. For example, if we read a fictional story, they only wanted to relate it to other stories. But I wanted them to also remember the news article we read on the same topic. Especially at the beginning of the year, it is important to provide more support and guiding questions to help your students make those connections.

Text-to-Text Connections Guide

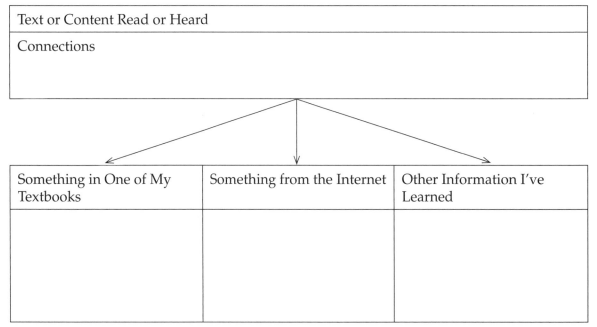

You can also adapt this to ask students to find supporting research or evidence for a thesis or main point of view. Other graphics similar to the text connection guide may be found by searching for "mind maps" on the internet.

Tool 76
Biopoems

Angie Wiggins uses poetry in her social studies classroom. When she teaches a unit about ancient Egypt, students read a myth about Osiris and Isis. After reading the myth, they write a biopoem about one of the Egyptian deities. The biopoem requires that students explain the feelings, fears, and desires of the god the student chose. After writing the poem, the students translate it into hieroglyphics.

God's Name

God of _____

Who feels _____(3 things)

Who fears _____(4 things)

Who would like to see _____

Resident of _____

God's Name

Sample Student Biopoem

Isis

Goddess of the dead

Who feels kindness toward everyone, love for her son, and happiness

Who fears Set, death of her or her family, and not finding Osiris's body

Who would like to see Egypt at peace

Resident of Egypt

Isis

Tool 77
Poetry and Vocabulary Concepts

You can use other types of poetry to reinforce learning. I recommend a haiku, the Japanese patterned three-line poem. Line one must include five syllables, line two, seven syllables, and line three, five syllables. It provides a different challenge for students to analyze information, then condense it and present it following the pattern. Sample haikus are on the next page.

Sample Haikus

Catalyst of life
Makes plants stronger and greener
Photosynthesis

Commas are our friend
They add meaning to our thoughts
We use them often

Seasons all mixed up
Is global warming a myth?
Our actions change earth

Recently, there was an article in *The New York Times* about a blogger who encourages the use of the Fibonacci sequence to write poems. It is an engaging way to explain math terms, while reinforcing a math concept.

Sample Fibonacci Sequence Poem

Divisibility

1 Math

1 house

2 divide

3 whole numbers

5 remainder zero

8 when the last digit is even

5 Then divide by 2

3 The answer

2 Should be

1A

1 Whole

Amber, Grade 7

A final way to make vocabulary more memorable is to have students develop concrete poems to help them remember the meaning of the word. Concrete poetry allows your students to be creative and use visuals. This is more motivating to your students who don't always feel successful with language. Since they must use words that describe or define the term or concept in order to create the picture, it is more challenging than it first appears.

Sample Concrete Poem

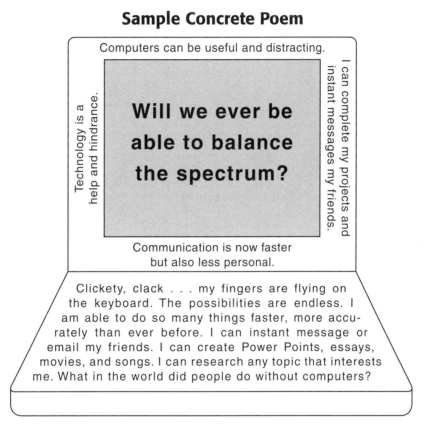

Computers can be useful and distracting.

Technology is a help and hindrance.

Will we ever be able to balance the spectrum?

I can complete my projects and instant messages my friends.

Communication is now faster but also less personal.

Clickety, clack . . . my fingers are flying on the keyboard. The possibilities are endless. I am able to do so many things faster, more accurately than ever before. I can instant message or email my friends. I can create Power Points, essays, movies, and songs. I can research any topic that interests me. What in the world did people do without computers?

Another Sample Concrete Poem

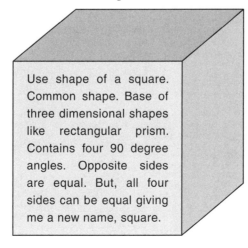

Use shape of a square. Common shape. Base of three dimensional shapes like rectangular prism. Contains four 90 degree angles. Opposite sides are equal. But, all four sides can be equal giving me a new name, square.

Tool 78
Put Yourself in Someone Else's Shoes

Another way to ratchet up the rigor of a standard assignment is to "Put Yourself in Someone Else's Shoes." Rather than simply researching a historical figure, character, or job role and writing a paper on the topic, ask students to truly step into the person's shoes. Students can create a fake Facebook wall or blog for the person, requiring them to move beyond basic information to reflect the person's thoughts, actions, life events, and feelings. I overheard one student say, "Making a Facebook wall for Martin Luther King, Jr. was a lot harder than I thought it would be. I kept having to go back and get more information."

Tool 79
Presentations

You can also enhance the rigor of student work by asking students to present information on a topic or concept. This also teaches real-life skills of organizing information, speaking, and confidence. Students can also incorporate technology, whether it is PowerPoint, video, or a Prezi. Be clear about your expectations for the presentation, and provide a rubric for grading or evaluating that matches your expectations.

PRESENT Acrostic

Points are clear and understandable
Resources
Each part flows within presentation
Style
Energy provided through interaction
New information
Thorough presentation of content

Tool 80
Virtual Tours

Another effective way to use technology in the classroom is to conduct virtual field trips. In today's budget-conscious schools, this is particularly helpful. Imagine the activities you can integrate into the classroom with a virtual tour of the Smithsonian.

However, it's important to remember that the field trip itself should not be the end result. Any tour should be linked to your standards, and the activities should result in increased learning related to your objectives. In the sample below, a visit to the Louvre was linked to a study of Egyptian history in grade 6. With adaptations of the assignments, it could easily be used in a high school art class.

The Louvre Visit

Today we are going to take an exciting trip to Paris, France! Your ticket is www.louvre.fr/en and your vehicle is your computer, tablet, or phone. Please read the instructions carefully so your trip is not wasted. I want you to have fun and learn something new in the process. We will have a round-table discussion on our magnificent trip on Friday. Have fun and I can't wait to hear about your adventure!

1. As your tour guide, I suggest you learn some information about the Louvre Museum because you begin your tour. Start at the *Collection and Louvre Palace* link. *Read the information about the history of The Louvre. You are in Paris and you call home to talk to someone your love. Tell them about the Louvre's history in 3–5 sentences. Include why the museum was established and how it has been important to France.*

2. Now you are ready to take your tour. Using the same link go to *Online Tours.* Choose following tour: **Egyptian Antiquities,** *Walk around on the floor to several areas. Spend 10 minutes learning how to navigate through the museum floor. Go to the help menu for ways to better navigate the tour.*

3. Choose one sculpture from your tour. Analyze how it reflects the culture of Egypt.

4. Interpret the artwork. Communicate the artist's statement. Describe what you think the artist is trying to say through the work of art. Expound on the feeling conveyed by the artwork. Describe what the artwork means to you, and why. Explain what you feel is the artist's intended purpose for creating that particular work of art. Examine why the artist made the choices in technique, materials and subject matter and how they relate to the intended purpose. Your narrative should be approximately one page.

Note: For more suggestions, visit www.wikihow.com/Critique-Artwork (the suggestions in number 4 are an excerpt from this site).

Ideas for Other Content Areas

Math: Students can plan the trip to the Louvre, look up the flight, and calculate the cost.

Social Studies: Plan what to take and how to pack, discuss how to prepare to visit the country, learn about Paris, and the French government. Also discuss the history of Egypt and the symbolism of the historical time period. Language Arts: How did the authors and poets of Egypt impact the culture? Also teach about critiques and writing the analysis.

Tool 81
Video Conferencing

As an alternative to "visiting" another place, you can bring expertise into the classroom. A variety of tools provide for video conferencing, in which you can bring a guest speaker into your classroom. Integrated as a part of an effective lesson, it can enhance learning and supplement your teaching. Be sure to test your equipment and internet connection in advance, as well as planning an alternative should the conference fail due to technical issues. In addition, coordinate the video conference within your instruction for the most effective learning experience for your students.

Tips for Effective Use of Video Conferencing

Find the right speaker—he or she should be an expert on his or her topic, as well as being an engaging speaker.

Find the right topic—some subjects lend themselves to a guest speaker, such as asking an engineer to speak to a career/technology class.

Find the right time—speakers can either motivate students to learn more about a topic or add to the lesson after your instruction.

Tool 82
Webquests

Webquests are lessons in which most or all of the content is web-based. All activities are inquiry-based, with a focus on higher order thinking. Webquests can be designed on almost any topic, including time capsules for a specific period, character exploration, bias and persuasion, or profiles of countries. You can create your own, or there are many published ones on the internet; simply conduct a search for webquest and your topic. If you are building your own, there are several steps to keep in mind that students will follow throughout the Webquest.

Typical Steps in a Webquest

Introduction

Task

Process

Evaluation

Conclusion

References

Working with Other Students

In a rigorous and engaging classroom, students work together for learning. Working with other students provides the opportunity for students to see and hear different perspectives, and to learn more effectively.

Tool 83
Clear Expectations

For any activities in which students are expected to work together, you'll want to provide clear expectations. In Chapter Seven, I provide a rubric for assessment of group work, but for now, there are four keys for effective group work.

First, show students what "good" collaboration looks like. Jessica Neuberger uses this process to prepare social studies students for their first student-led portfolio assessment conferences. As she explains:

I recorded a sample interview to give the students a good idea of what to expect. When the class viewed the sample interview, I would stop the video after each question, have the students repeat each question to me and then they would write it down. The second time through, we watched the whole interview with no interruptions. Then we discussed it. When I interviewed the students throughout the next week, they were prepared to share their work with me, offer me their opinions of their strengths and weaknesses, and we were able to set a goal for the next part of the year.

Because she knew this would be challenging for her students, she modeled the entire process for them and then provided scaffolded instruction to ensure their success.

Tool 84
Group Members' Roles

Next, explain what their individual roles are, and be sure each understands what he or she is to do in his or her role.

Sample Roles

Facilitator—leader of the group; facilitates action

Recorder—records comments and/or work

Reporter—reports work to the entire group

Materials manager—collects and distributes materials

Time keeper—keeps the group working within time limits

Wildcard—assistant to the leader; fills in holes

Encourager—encourages others

Summarizer—summarizes work and may report to the class

Fact checker—checks work from group; researches facts

Reflector—reflects on comments from group, asks probing questions

Designer—designs the project

Creator—creates or builds the design

Third, provide guides and/or planning tools to help with the assignment. This might include the steps for the activities, or processes students should follow. You may ask students to collaborate in class, or use wikis to coordinate their work during out-of-class times.

Tool 85
Self-Assessment

Finally, provide opportunities for self-assessment. This will facilitate more peer collaboration, and also encourage reflection, a higher level thinking skill.

Self-Assessment

S—Did I help **solve** the problem or complete the assignment?

E—Did I **engage** with other members in a positive way?

L—What did I **learn** from working with others?

F—Did I **follow** through on my role, as well as helping others?

Tool 86
Student Discourse

An important tool to use in all classes and grade levels is discourse, or student talk. As Natalie House explains:

I strongly encourage my students to discuss topics. I find when they do, they internalize the concepts. I find it better when they can discuss to develop a new concept rather than my just telling them. Often, I will pose a problem, have the students work on it individually or in pairs. After they have had some time, I will have them discuss it with a partner.

Then, I will bring the whole class together to discuss. I want students to feed off each other and discuss without my being involved too much. If I think students will have a hard time discussing, I have them write down a few discussion points before we begin.

One caution is that all student talk is not discourse. In rigorous discourse, students not only are talking about the topic at hand, they are doing so at higher levels. You may want to provide structure with guiding questions. And, although your role shifts to facilitator, you will find you need to actively listen.

LISTEN Acrostic

Listen to students continually.

Inspire questions through your modeling and guidance.

Students should ask and discuss answers to questions.

Talk prompts may be provided if needed.

Evaluate and provide feedback.

Nudge students when they are stuck.

Tool 87
Debates

In order to help students analyze an issue from two or more sides, use debates as a teaching tool. Lindsay Yearta uses debates to teach her students to see different perspectives on an issue. She begins with a handout that includes a statement: "I am for/against (insert your topic here)." Next, she assigns each student a position (for or against). The students circle their position on a handout and then research three reasons to support their position. She says:

They get into their groups and come up with what they think the other group would say. What do you think their points are going to be? Then, they write down at least three points their opposition might have and they research comebacks to the opposition's points. So, they have to think ahead and research not only their position, but the other side as well. Then, when we hold our debate, each student had to speak at least once.

The verbal exchange is supported by the depth of research on both points of view. Barbara D. Martin (http://kiwiyert.tripod.com/ideas_for_debate_topics.htm) shares ideas for debate topics.

Sample Debate Topics

Should students be required to wear school uniforms?

Should you be allowed to go anywhere you want with your friends?

Should you be given an allowance or an increase in your allowance?

Should you be permitted to have a pet?

Should you be allowed to have your ears or other body parts pierced?

Should you be allowed to get a tattoo?

Should you be required to wear mandatory bicycle helmets?

Should you have homework every night?

Should skateboards be allowed on sidewalks?

Computers should replace teachers.

Girls have it better than boys.

If you would like exemplars for debate positions, you can use editorials and opposing columns. For example, *USA Today* regularly publishes an opposing view to their editorial.

Tool 88
Thinking Hats

Still another way to help students think about a topic from a variety of perspectives is through the use of Thinking Hats (DeBono, 1999). The process provides six different ways of viewing or discussing information and is helpful anytime you want students to look at something through different lenses.

Thinking Hats

The White Hat calls for information known or needed. "The facts, just the facts."

The Yellow Hat symbolizes brightness and optimism. Under this hat you explore the positives and probe for value and benefit.

The Black Hat is judgment—the devil's advocate or why something may not work. Spot the difficulties and dangers—where things might go wrong. Probably the most powerful and useful of the hats but a problem if overused.

The Red Hat signifies feelings, hunches and intuition. When using this hat you can express emotions and feelings and share fears, likes, dislikes, loves, and hates.

The Green Hat focuses on creativity—the possibilities, alternatives, and new ideas. It's an opportunity to express new concepts and new perceptions.

The Blue Hat is used to manage the thinking process. It's the control mechanism that ensures the Six Thinking Hats® guidelines are observed.

Source: www.debonogroup.com/6hats.htm

Kendra Alston uses Thinking Hats to help in the brainstorming process of argumentative (problem/solution) writing. "The students had to think of a problem and used the Thinking Hats strategy as a way to help them elaborate/support and as a way to organize their essays. We also used it in Class Meeting as a type of conflict resolution strategy." You could also use Thinking Hats in debates to connect thinking and speaking.

Tool 89
Problem-Based Learning

Problem-based learning is "an inquiry process that resolves questions . . . Student inquiry is very much an integral part of PBL and problem resolution" (John Barell, 2006, p. 3).

You may be thinking that PBL sounds a lot like project-based learning. The main difference is that in project-based learning, the teacher directs the questions and assigns the final product. In problem-based learning, the students are more self-directed and come up with many of their own questions. This learning process aligns seamlessly with the CCSS in Writing that require students to research to build and present knowledge.

I recently visited a kindergarten classroom using PBL. Students were learning about various colors, and one student asked, "Are there other colors we don't know about?" The teacher took advantage of this question, and asked students to work with a partner to create their own colors. Students had total flexibility with how they determined their color, how they would explain the color to the class, and how they would show and/or demonstrate the new color. As one student said to me, "It was awesome to answer our own question!"

Darrin Baird used problem-based learning with his high school marketing students. As he said, "I turned the control to students, rather than me." One day, he brought a box of Cheerios to class. As he discussed marketing ideas for different products, the students began to plan other purposes for Cheerios. They worked in small groups to discover purposes for the cereal, as well as ways to market the product. This open-ended activity enabled students to solve a complex problem of interest to them that was also linked to their class standards.

Tool 90
Speed Booking

An adaptation of speed dating, speed booking (see Moen, 2007) allows students to share books and articles they have read. Simply pair students together, and they explain to each other the key details of the book or article they've read. You can also use this with a video they watched, such as YouTube videos on a topic. After they share, they move to a new partner, until they have had the chance to share three to five times.

After a short introduction, they focus on key aspects of their text (see samples below), citing specific evidence for their opinions. Notice that although some of the questions are basic who or what items, they are always followed by higher level applications.

Questions for Fiction	Questions for Non-Fiction
Who is the most interesting character?	What were the main points of the text?
What exemplifies the character (phrase, action, etc.)?	What perspective/opinion did the author have?
What key events happened during the story/video?	How did the author express his/her opinion?
Why were they important?	Was the article/text factual?
How did the events lead up to the conclusion?	How do you know?

This activity is also adaptable for research conducted on a topic. Each student can use a different source of information for the topic, and then share with each other.

Tool 91
Jigsaw

One year when I was teaching ninth grade, I was assigned to teach a photography class. This was a challenge because it was not my area of expertise. In fact, it wasn't even a hobby; but there was a need for a teacher and I had an extra class period. The first half of the course was to be the history of photography. You can imagine how excited ninth graders were about that!

Rather than lecturing the entire time, I used the jigsaw method of group work. Students are assigned to small groups (I used groups of four). Next, students number themselves in the groups. Each student will become an expert on a particular topic. All students who are numbered one move together to study their assigned area. Students who are number two do the same, as do numbers three and four. A key part of working in the larger groups is that members agree on the most important aspects of their topic. Third, the "experts" return to their original groups of four students. In turn, each expert teaches his or her subject to his or her small group. Finally, the teacher leads a whole group discussion of the topics.

You can use this anytime you would like to have students teach each other. In my son's science class, his teacher split up a chapter in the book, and each of the expert groups created a rap to teach their smaller groups. Not only was it engaging, but also students were required to use higher order skills to create a rap that represented the content. As another alternative, you can also have "expert" groups create multimedia presentations that can be shared with their individual groups.

Jigsaw in Ten Easy Steps

1. Divide students into five- or six-person jigsaw groups. The groups should be diverse in terms of gender, ethnicity, race, and ability.

2. Appoint one student from each group as the leader. Initially, this person should be the most mature student in the group.

3. Divide the day's lesson into five or six segments. For example, if you want history students to learn about Eleanor Roosevelt, you might divide a short biography of her into standalone segments on: (1) Her childhood; (2) Her family life with Franklin and their children; (3) Her life after Franklin contracted polio; (4) Her work in the White House as First Lady; and (5) Her life and work after Franklin's death.

4. Assign each student to learn one segment, making sure students have direct access only to their own segment.

5. Give students time to read over their segment at least twice and become familiar with it. There is no need for them to memorize it.

6. Form temporary "expert groups" by having one student from each jigsaw group join other students assigned to the same segment. Give students in these expert groups time to discuss the main points of their segment and to rehearse the presentations they will make to their jigsaw group.

7. Bring the students back into their jigsaw groups.

8. Ask each student to present her or his segment to the group. Encourage others in the group to ask questions for clarification.

9. Float from group to group, observing the process. If any group is having trouble (e.g., a member is dominating or disruptive), make an appropriate intervention. Eventually, it's best for the group leader to handle this task. Leaders can be trained by whispering an instruction on how to intervene, until the leader gets the hang of it.

10. At the end of the session, give a quiz on the material so that students quickly come to realize that these sessions are not just fun and games but really count.

Source: www.jigsaw.org/steps.htm

Tool 92
Paideia Seminars

A type of group discussion is a Paideia seminar, which shifts the role of the teacher to that of a facilitator and emphasizes each student's contribution to the discussion. Prior to the seminar, students prepare usually through reading. After the seminar, students apply the ideas and values, typically through writing.

As Marcia Alexander, a high school teacher explains:

Paideia seminar has been the most successful teaching tool that I have used because it gives students the opportunity to demonstrate their knowledge and concerns about an issue that they can relate to. For example, I may have students read an excerpt written by Sojourner Truth, an African American ex-female slave, abolitionist, and speaker of women rights. The discussion topic is discrimination and I create open-ended questions, such as "Does being illiterate make a person less intelligent?"

In her role as a facilitator, Marcia ensures that every student speaks at least once before she poses another open-ended question. The nature of the discussion requires that students actively listen to each other in order to respond appropriately.

Real-Life Learning Applications

Ideally, students should see real-life applications to the majority, if not all, of their learning. However, that is more difficult than it sounds. Too often, students say, "I have to learn this because it's on the test" or "I have to learn this because the teacher said so." Those are not relevant to students, and it often does not motivate them. Although many of the activities we've looked at include real-life applications, in this section, we'll look at some specific strategies to incorporate these applications.

Tool 93
Simulations

Simulations are re-creations or adaptations of authentic events. They are effective for giving students a more realistic experience, and for helping them understand a situation at higher levels.

Max Fischer, a National Board Certified Teacher, shared his favorite simulation with Education World (www.educationworld.com/a_curr/curr391.shtml).

I called it The King's M & Ms. In order to get my students to realize how American colonists really felt about King George's Stamp Act and the subsequent Intolerable Acts, which taxed various imported goods such as tea, I gave each student ten M&Ms in a paper cup. I randomly assigned roles where most students were colonists, two were tax collectors, two were members of Parliament, and one was King George. Members of Parliament drew slips of paper out of a hat on which I had written down the names of some common items. These items—for example, blue jeans, Nike shoes, or eyeglasses—would be subject to taxation. The tax collectors came around and withdrew a specific number of candy pieces for each taxable item if a student possessed that item. The confiscated candies were distributed among Parliament members and the king (with a few going to the tax collectors). The student colonists were infuriated, and I compared their umbrage of the apparent inequity in candy distribution to what the colonists actually felt toward the British system of taxation. The fact that the students had no say in what was taxed in the classroom paralleled the infamous "taxation without representation" sentiment of the colonists.

Tool 94
RAFT

Perhaps you would like your students to write a paragraph about the topic you have been teaching in class, such as the solar system. That is a standard, low-level assignment that requires students to restate or summarize the information covered. Even if you ask students to elaborate in greater detail, it's likely that the responses are fairly basic. Instead, let's ratchet up the rigor using the RAFT strategy (Santa, Havens, & Macumber, 1996).

RAFT stands for Role/Audience/Format/Topic. Using this strategy, students would assume a role (such as an astronaut in this case) and write from that perspective to a more authentic audience, such as people reading his/her online blog. With a slight shift in the assignment details, students are required to understand the topic at a higher level in order to complete the task. Additionally, when students are asked to write for a genuine purpose and audience, they tend to complete the assignment more effectively. As you can see from the examples, you can tailor this task to your specific needs. For younger students, they can draw rather than write their RAFTs. Also, choose roles and formats that interest them.

RAFT Examples

Role	Audience	Format	Topic
White Blood Cell	Red Blood Cell	Map	Circulatory System
Quotation Marks	Author	Persuasive Speech	How I Can Help You Write a Novel
Square Root	Whole Number	Rap/Song	Explain Relationship

see next page

RAFT Examples

Role	Audience	Format	Topic
Lawyer	US Supreme Court	Appeal Speech	Dred Scott Decision
Chef	Television Audience	Script	Wonders of eggs
Treble Clef	Students	Commercial	Purpose
Child	Parent	Dinner Conversation	Facebook as an Educational Tool

Tool 95
Critiques

Another important skill students need to learn is to critique a piece of work, whether it is a text, piece of art or music, or a performance. This ties very nicely to the Common Core's expectation of analyzing a work and providing evidence of your analysis. In a critique, students must evaluate the work, and detail specific examples to support their opinion. The sample critique guidelines provide additional direction.

Critique Guidelines

Consider each aspect of the piece/project.

Reflect on your initial thoughts/perspectives.

Identify specific examples that support your perspective.

Think about the author's/creator's perspective.

Include other possible considerations.

Question why the author might have included those examples.

Unify your thoughts.

Evaluate the overall piece.

Tool 96
Gallery Walk

An ideal way to apply the critique activity is through gallery walks. After students create a work, such as a science project, create a gallery of the finished products. Students walk through the gallery, and are assigned three specific works. They critique the works using the guidelines above, then compare the three samples. This allows a real-life audience for the completed projects, and also provides a practical opportunity for students to practice writing critiques.

Opportunities for Review

The closing of a lesson is a key part of understanding. If there is not an opportunity to reflect upon and summarize learning, students will often leave a lesson without truly understanding what they should know. There are easy ways to review lessons.

Tool 97
Songs, Raps, and Riddles

One way to kick up reviews is to ask students to explain concepts or vocabulary in a more rigorous and engaging manner. Having your students create their own songs, raps, or riddles requires them to apply concepts and think at higher levels. The New York Times holds a contest for students to write a rap about the year. Below, you'll see a sample from one of the winners.

Rap About 2011 by Satat O

2011, according to the Chinese, the Year of Rabbit,

Meaning it is the year of being calm, but the opposite happened.

Like we had Irene, which was a deadly scene in the west,

In Middle East we have the Navy give Bin to Death.

Strange how this happened when Barack was getting less respect,

Chances dwindle for Perry because unfortunately he forgets.

The tsunami water tyrant hits the Japanese island, sadly,

Record number of tornados in the US, not just in the alley.

Rebels wanted Gadaffhi's blood, and now they have their hunger eased,

The soldiers return from the war that had troubled peace.

But the world still isn't well; our economy isn't making a recovery,

The blame goes on Wall Street and overspent celebrity luxuries.

The last space shuttle lands and not another to make discoveries.

Add the digits in 2011, you get four, in Chinese that means death,

Like the casualties, Laden, Jobs, Gadhafi, the war, and the shuttle program, what's next?

Source: http://learning.blogs.nytimes.com/2012/01/13/student-contest-winners-the-2011-year-in-rap/

Tool 98
Reflective Journals

Another way to help your students review as well as become more independent learners is through the use of reflective journals or personal blogs. I regularly ask students to take a minute to write down what they learned and, more importantly, how they know they understand the content. I want to make sure they do more than just write down a few facts; I want them to understand *why* they understand! You can do this at the end of each learning activity or you can have them write periodically.

Sample Reflective Questions

What have I learned that's important?

How will it help me academically, personally, and/or in my real life?

What contributed to my learning?

What particular assignments, or activities really helped me learn?

What questions do I still have? How can I learn this information?

Tool 99
Pizza Wheel

I also use a pizza wheel during class to review chunks of material students are assigned to read prior to or during class. Each student writes a fact he or she learned in one of the pizza slices. Then, working in small groups, students rotate their papers to the next group member, who also writes a fact. This continues around the circle until each pizza is full. As an alternative, students can write examples of evidence that supports an opinion or perspective. Students then discuss the material, using the pizza wheels as a prompt. Although you can measure students' understanding in an oral discussion, asking each student to write ensures that all students are involved in the lesson and provides an opportunity for every student to respond.

Sample Pizza Wheel

Student: _____

Topic: _____ *Volcanos* _____

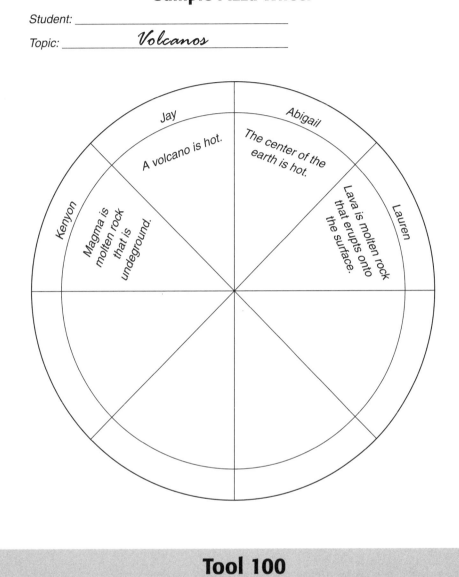

Tool 100
Exit Slips

Another easy way to review student learning and also assess student understanding is through the use of exit slips (see Chapter Seven for more on assessing student understanding). As students are leaving your class, they complete a paper or index cards responding to three statements:

Exit Slip

What I learned today: _____

_____

How this connects to something else I know: _____

_____

A question I still have: _____

_____

Not only does this allow students to reflect of their knowledge from the day, it also encourages critical thinking to narrow down their answers to one for each question. If you'd prefer, you can collect the exit slips through technology, such as online surveys, email, or responses on a class blog/wiki/Facebook page.

Tool 101
Read the Room

Applicable to many of the strategies suggested, Read the Room allows students to review materials from other students' perspectives. For any small group summaries, charts, diagrams, etc. that students complete, post them around the room. Either at the end of the lesson or at the beginning of the next day, students rotate through the posted material, "reading the room." This can spur discussion, or if you'd like, you can have students do an exit slip analyzing and synthesizing what they've read.

Conclusion

There are a limitless number of strategies you can use to enhance your instruction and make it more rigorous. Increasing student engagement, ensuring all students participate in learning, and encouraging higher order thinking should be an integral part of all activities.

Reflection into Action

1. What are three main tools from this chapter you could use in your classroom?

2. Which of those three will you put into place in the next three days?

3. Are there any resources you need to make this happen?

4. Which one would you like to implement next week?

5. What other tools do you want to consider for the future?

6. Is there anything else from this chapter you want to remember after you finish the book?

5
Give Support

As you increase rigor for your students, you must also increase the level of support they receive. Consider a time when you tried to accomplish something new. For example, think about your first year of teaching. Did you need help or guidance? That's exactly how our students are as they move to higher levels of rigor. However, you don't want to provide the same level of support all the time.

> Gradual Release
>
> Scaffolding (Before, During, and After Lessons)
>
> Differentiation
>
> Working with Special Populations

Gradual Release

It's important to realize that support should be used at an appropriate level through the learning process. At the beginning of more rigorous learning, more support is needed. However, as the learning continues, we want students to become more independent in their learning.

Tool 102
Bicycle Model

When I was a young girl, I wanted to ride a bike. However, I had to start with a tricycle. I needed to be close to the ground, and I needed the support of extra wheels. However, after a couple of years, I was ready to ride a children's bicycle. Of course, it had training wheels, because I still needed the balance of two additional wheels at the back. Next, I remember the day my father took off the training wheels so I could ride without them. He still held on to the back of the seat, to make sure I learned how to keep my balance without the extra wheels. Finally, he let go of the seat and let me ride by myself, one of the proudest days of my young life.

97

That's one way to think of scaffolding. At the beginning of a new concept, students may need strong, consistent support so they don't falter. Then, lessen the support a bit, but still ensure that you have built in the scaffolding strategies. Next, pull back a bit, but still stay close by to make sure they are successful. Lastly, they'll try it by themselves and show they understand the concept without your help.

Tool 103
Me, Us, You Diamond

A second way to think about scaffolding is with a diamond. As you can see from the diamond below, it starts with me (meaning the teacher). You begin by modeling a lesson. Next, we go to us. There are two parts of this. First is the teacher and the students (us) following guided practice. The second part of guided practice is us, meaning students working with partners or in small groups. Finally, the student (you) does the work independently.

Me, Us, You Diamond

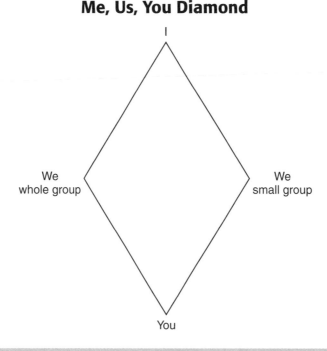

Tool 104
Concrete, Representational, Abstract

A third method that is particularly helpful in math instruction is to consider students working through a concept at a concrete level, then a representation level, then the abstract. Although Brad Witzel (Blackburn and Witzel, 2013) provides an example for elementary school, the process is applicable at all levels.

Let's look at an example of how an interventionist used CRA to help a second grader under-stand addition and subtraction to 100. Jacob thought that he was simply "bad at math"

Concrete, Representational, Abstract Examples

Concrete	Pictorial Representation	Abstract
		$+\ 40\ +\ 5$ $+\ 10\ +\ 8$ $+\ 50\ +\ 13$ $=\ +\ 63$

and incapable of succeeding. At the end of his first grade, his teacher marked his report card as acceptable but identified to his parents that he struggled throughout the year. Since math typically builds in successive increments, Jacob's first grade struggles were bound to cause trouble in second. Jacob knew this as well as his parents and the teachers. Placing him in math intervention in second grade was a great way to help. The second grade interventionist, Miriam, recalled, "Knowing that I couldn't dive into the second grade curriculum, I worked some explicit CRA methods with first grade standards, such as addition and subtraction to 20. He had attempted this content a long time back but he never really understood it. By covering the old content and teaching Jacob the first grade standard again allowed him to generalize the approach to the lesson in second grade, adding and subtracting to 100. By teaching him the concepts, he was able to transfer the skills of one grade level into the next. The tier 1 teacher was so impressed with his performance and so excited by his resulting enthusiasm that he was asked to present his approach to the class.

Scaffolding

Scaffolding is one type of support that you offer to students. There is a variety of strategies to use, which we will consider in the context of those that are useful before the lesson, during the lesson, and after the lesson.

Before Lesson Strategies

Before teaching the lesson, there are several aspects we'll want to consider. Let's take a look at prior knowledge, vocabulary, and modeling. These can all provide a strong foundation for learning.

Content Prior Knowledge

Content-based prior knowledge is the knowledge base students bring to a lesson about the specific topic.

Tool 105
Anticipatory Guide

It's important to determine what a student actually understands about a concept prior to instruction. Pat Vining, a math teacher, uses a simple activity to check her students' prior knowledge of the concept and to clear up any misunderstandings students may have about the topic. First, she gives students three minutes to answer a short true/false questionnaire. Next, in pairs, students compare responses and use the textbook to check their answers. Each set of partners must rewrite any false statements so that they are true. She ends with a whole-class discussion to ensure understanding.

Sample Anticipatory Guide—Pythagorean Theorem

Directions: Check whether the statement is true or false.

_____ 1. The longest side of a triangle is called the hypotenuse.

_____ 2. In the Pythagorean theorem, the variable c stands for the hypotenuse.

_____ 3. Any side in a right triangle is called a leg.

_____ 4. A corollary is a statement that can be easily proved using a theorem.

_____ 5. If you know the lengths of all three sides of a right triangle, you can use the Pythagorean theorem to determine whether it is a right triangle.

Tool 106
K-W-L

Probably the most common method of identifying students' prior knowledge that I see in classrooms today is a K-W-L chart. During a K-W-L activity, you ask the students what they already know about a topic (K) or what they think they know about it. Next, you ask what they want to know (W). Then, you teach the lesson and ask them what they learned (L). You can also add an H—How Can We Learn This to create a K-W-H-L organizer.

K-W-H-L Chart

K (what I know or think I know)	W (what I want to learn)	H (how I can learn this)	L (what I learned)

Tool 107
LINK Strategy

Kendra Alston adapts the K-W-L strategy into a LINK for her students (overleaf).

LINK Chart

L (list everything you know)	I (inquire about what you want to know)	N (now we are going to take notes)	K (what do you know now?)

After they complete the L column individually, her students turn to a partner and share their answers. Then, she leads a short class discussion, charting out what everyone in the class knows about the topic. As she works through the lesson, students finish by writing what they now know (K), and they tear that part off to turn in as they leave her class. This provides her immediate feedback as to what her students learned or didn't learn in class.

It's important to share students' responses with everyone, albeit it in a safe way that doesn't embarrass anyone. That's why I like her method. She starts by allowing each student to write an individual response, so everyone has an opportunity to think about what they know. As Kendra points out, if I'm a student:

[B]*y sharing with a partner, I can feel "safer" in case I'm not right. In the whole class discussion, I'm sharing "our" answers (mine and my partner's), so I don't feel like I'm out on a limb by myself. You could even add another option of sharing with two groups of partners before you share with everyone. However, don't sacrifice the whole class discussion. We all learn more together, and it's a safe guess that someone in my class knows something I don't know. Listening to all responses and charting them out for everyone to see helps me build prior knowledge when I don't have much.*

Strategic Prior Knowledge

A second type of prior knowledge is strategic knowledge. This is the knowledge students have about learning strategies, such as listening or working together.

Tool 108
Paying Attention

For example, if your students are not paying attention, you can teach your students the SLANT model. By learning the SLANT model, students learn how to appear like they are paying attention, and, in turn, may improve their actual academic engaged time.

SLANT

Sit up

Lean forward

Act attentive using varied facial expressions

Nod when the person pauses, and

Track the speaker maintaining intermittent eye contact.

Source: Ellis, 1991

Tool 109
Note-Taking

A strategy that many students struggle with is that of taking notes. And, as teachers, we may assume students know how to take notes. Too often, students either write down everything they see or hear, or they write nothing down. Unfortunately, neither is effective.

Today, we often use PowerPoint to put notes up on a screen. However, students simply copy the PowerPoint. This isn't note-taking; again, this is copying. It's important to teach students how to take notes. Although this may take time, you will reap the benefits later. I recommend the ten-step process below.

Steps for Teaching Note-Taking

1. Discuss the importance of taking notes.
2. Point out that taking notes is writing some of what is written or said.
3. Use a PowerPoint slide to show a section of text.
4. Model identifying three to five key words or phrases to write down.
5. Demonstrate how to write additional notes or an explanation without looking at the screen.
6. Ask students to do the next screen on their own.
7. Provide additional modeling and guided practice as needed.
8. Ask students to practice note-taking during a lesson.
9. Provide feedback as to the quality of the notes.
10. Remind students as needed of the appropriate way to take notes.

Tool 110
Problem Solving

Another strategy is that of problem solving. There are several steps to solving a problem. The use of graphic organizers is particularly helpful. In the seventh grade example below, students work through the process of scientific inquiry (South Carolina Science Curriculum Standards Support Guide 7–1.3).

Problem Solving with a Scientific Inquiry

What are you testing?	• Create a testable questions. • Test one variable.
Reserach topic information	• Key fact 1 • Key fact 2 • Key fact 3
State Hypothesis	• What is a predicted answer to your question? • What may be the possible outcome of the investigation?
Design an experiment	• Control all variables except the independent variable. • Plan for independent and dependent variables with repeated trials. • Plan for factors that should be constant. • Plan for a control set-up. • List materials needed to conduct your experiment. • List procedures you will follow to conduct your experiment. • Record your data. • Organize your data. • Analyze your data.

Vocabulary

Vocabulary is another critical aspect of preparing for a lesson. Ideally, students understand new vocabulary from the context of their reading. However, in many cases, particularly for struggling students, this is not true. In those situations, you may need to pre-teach some vocabulary. Also consider that you may need to limit the number of words you are pre-teaching; the Common Core State Standards encourage close reading, which recommends students experience vocabulary initially in context.

Tool 111
Word Wheel

Annette Kimball, a high school Spanish teacher, designed a Word Wheel to help her students learn vocabulary. Rather than simply asking them to write the word, a definition, and a sentence, she added steps so they would look more in-depth at the meaning. Prior to defining the word, students were required to specify synonyms, antonyms and related words. You'll find the English translation below the wheel.

Sample Word Wheel

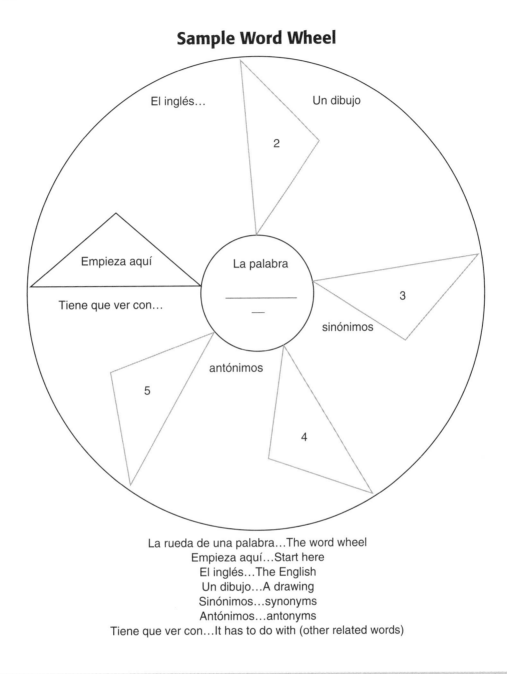

La rueda de una palabra…The word wheel
Empieza aquí…Start here
El inglés…The English
Un dibujo…A drawing
Sinónimos…synonyms
Antónimos…antonyms
Tiene que ver con…It has to do with (other related words)

Tool 112
Concept Map

Graphic organizers are one of the best ways to support students through vocabulary instruction. Giving them a picture that represents the vocabulary word helps them remember the concept, as well as helping them connect it to other pictures in their mind. In this sample, a music teacher helps his students understand the relationships of musical concepts.

Sample Concept Map

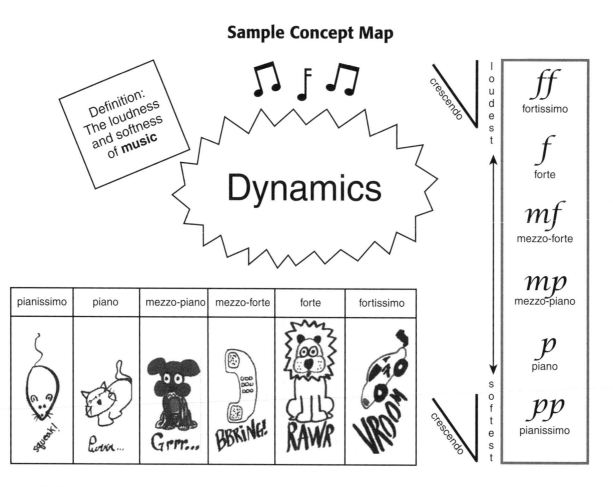

Modeling

A particular issue for many students is not knowing what good looks like. We ask students to complete a process or an assignment, and we are frustrated when the quality of work does not match our expectations. This leads us to question whether or not the student cares about doing the work or wonder if the student tried at all. But, many of our most frustrated—and frustrating—students simply don't know what to do, how to do it, or they think what they are doing is right.

That's why modeling is so important. By showing students what to do and how to do it, they will be more successful.

Tool 113
Digital Literacy

Reading on the internet is different from reading a book or story. Rather than having a standard structure to the text, students jump from page to page, effectively creating their own set of information. They also must deal with distractions, whether in the form of pop-ups or ads. There is also some research that students tend to scan more when reading on the internet.

There are several important strategies to model for students reading electronic articles and sources. Although they are similar to those for traditional texts, they become more important with internet sources.

Find the source of the information.

Determine if the source is credible.

Scan the entire article to get an overview.

Ignore the distracters on the page.

Don't click away unless you have a good reason to do so.

Look for key words.

Read the article thoroughly.

Go back and look for answers to specific questions—What is the main point? What is the evidence to support the thesis?

Tool 114
Assignments

Modeling is also needed when you expect students to complete a process, a higher-order task, or a project. This often occurs when you ask students to answer questions or complete a project that requires more than just reciting facts, such as describing the causes of an event in history, persuading the reader of a position, or explaining how to solve a math problem. Each type of question requires higher-level thinking skills and applying all those facts they memorized.

Chances are, your at-risk students don't do well with these types of questions or similar assignments such as reports or projects. Again, don't assume that it's because they don't want to or just aren't doing it. Many students simply don't know how to do this correctly. As teachers, it is our job to activate or provide background knowledge with content, as well as process. Let's look at a framework for making performance expectations explicit with higher-level assignments. In our case, we'll look at asking students to write an extended response, or essay-type answer.

Start by discussing the assignment with students: "One task you'll need to complete to be successful in my class is to answer essay questions appropriately. How many of you have written answers to essay questions before?" "What did you have to do to make a good grade on them?" Discuss the answers, clarifying misconceptions. Most of the time, you don't grade based on the number of sentences; that may reflect depth, but many times it doesn't.

Second, show a sample of a *good or acceptable* answer to a question. Be sure to tell students this is an example you would consider to be good. Have students read the sample or read it with them. Discuss what you are looking for in an answer. It's important that your expectations are clear. Before this class, decide on your key criteria for what makes a good answer, and state those in terms that are understandable to students.

Discuss what you are looking for: "Just as there are discipline rules in a school to ensure order and acceptable behavior, there are basic procedures to follow to be successful with learning. First, you need to answer the question. Sometimes students will put in extra information that doesn't answer the question, because they think they need more words or sentences. That can actually make your answer worse." Continue to describe other rules. "Just as a reminder, for the first few weeks of school, I will post the procedures." Show the poster on your wall that lists the criteria and provides visual reinforcement.

Third, gently discuss the differences between your procedures and their experiences. Don't tell your students they are wrong; explain that you want them to understand what they need to do to be successful in your class: "You'll notice that my rules are a little different from what you told me you did last year. Although you can't really answer my questions with just a sentence or two, I don't just count the number of words or sentences. I look at whether you actually answered the question, whether or not you gave at least three examples to support your answer, and so on. I know this may be a little different, so let's see what that actually looks like." Show a sample answer on the board, the overhead, or in a handout; and point out exactly how the sample meets your expectations. Be sure to give specific examples.

Fourth, give students another sample answer, preferably on a handout. Pair students and have them read the answer and decide whether or not it follows the rules. You might even have them guess the grade, but I usually start just with satisfactory or not satisfactory rather than A, B, or C. Lead a whole-class discussion, going to each of your rules and asking students whether or not the sample meets the rule and why or why not: "Let's talk about how this answer matches the criteria. The first guideline is that a question should answer the question. The question was [insert sample here]. Does this answer actually answer that?" Students respond. "Can you tell me where exactly in the essay it answers the question?" Again, allow students to respond.

Fifth, using the same process, provide a second example to give students another chance to practice looking for good responses. As they write their own answers, explain that they need to do the same things. If students are hung up on particular misconceptions such as always needing three paragraphs, give them a model that does so but is bad in other ways so they can see the difference in criteria.

Sixth, give them a question to answer, reminding them that they should complete the answer using your rules. Pick a simple question; your focus in this lesson is on the process of writing a good answer rather than demonstrating they understand new content. That is ultimately your desired result, but let's do the basics first. Remember, if students don't know where they want to go (a good response), they also don't know how to walk (how to get there).

Finally, have them either write down the guidelines from your poster or give them a writer's checklist to use as they complete their short essay. During the next lesson or the next day, review the rules with your students through an interactive discussion. As you go through each rule, ask them to look at their own essays to check if they followed the rule. Have them physically check each rule on the paper or the checklist. Then pair them up again to check each other's papers, again rule by rule, while you move around the room monitoring their work. Give them the chance to rewrite their answers before they turn them in for a grade.

Working through this process with your students takes several days and may need to be revisited throughout the year. Also, the use of rubrics supports this process. Providing students with a clear set of clarifying statements for each criterion on your procedures chart can help them improve their writing throughout the year.

Tool 115
Metacognitive Organizer

Prior to a lesson, it is helpful to provide an organizer for students' thinking. A simple K-W-L (see Tool 106 in this chapter) is one way to help students thinking about their own thinking. Another option is to model what students are expected to do through mnemonics, or acronyms that remind students of different strategies to use throughout their task.

FAST is a Mnemonic Device for Basic Problem Solving

Find what you're solving for.

Ask yourself, "What are the parts of the problem?"

Set up the numbers.

Take down the sign.

Source: http://floridarti.usf.edu/resources/topic/academic_support/ask/binder_materials/instr_strategies.pdf

---

Tool 116
Anticipation Guides

Another type of metacognitive modeling is to provide an advanced organizer for students. Anticipation guides are particularly helpful. We discussed one use in Tool 105 as a way to help activate prior knowledge. In this case, it is used during reading to help students process their thinking.

Sample Anticipation Guide 1

Topic or Chapter/Text		
My Thought or Prediction	**author's Point**	**Evidence or Page Number**

Adapted from www.readingrockets.org/strategies/anticipation_guide/

Anticipatory Guides can be used in any subject area.

Sample Anticipation Guide 2

Anticipation Guide   readwritethink
                                                                     Reading Association NCTE

Read each of the following statements. Then decide how strongly you agree or disagree with each. Explain your thinking in a sentence or two.

SA = Strongly Agree	A = Agree	D = Disagree	SD = Strongly Disagree

Statements	SA	A	D	SD	Explanations

After reading/discussing, look back at your ratings and explanations. Discuss how your thinking has changed or been confirmed on one or more of the statements.

Source: www.readwritethink.org/files/resources/printouts/AnticipationGuide.pdf

Tool 117
Characteristics of Effective Anticipation Guides

Ausubel, Novak, and Hanesian (1978) describe a more structured anticipatory guide. As you plan the guide, keep in mind the following steps. Additionally, students must be taught how to use the guide throughout their task.

Effective Anticipation Guides

♦ Inform the students of the use of an advance organizer.

♦ Identify the major topics and tasks.

♦ Provide an organizational framework.

♦ Clarify the action to be taken/completed.

♦ Provide background information.

♦ State concepts to be learned.

♦ Clarify concepts to be learned.

♦ Motivate students to learn through establishing relevance. Introduce and identify new vocabulary.

♦ State general outcomes and objectives to be mastered.

During Lesson

Some of the before lesson strategies, such as the anticipatory guides, can also be used during the lesson. For example, modeling should continue to occur throughout the lesson. Let's look at effective strategies to use in your instruction.

Tool 118
Think Alouds for Modeling

A useful modeling technique is a think-aloud. A think-aloud is a teacher verbalizing his or her thoughts and reasoning when solving a problem, making sense of text, or completing a task. In math, it may be explaining stepwise reasoning. (See the following example from Brad Witzel—Blackburn and Witzel, 2013.) In reading, it may be stopping during reading and checking comprehension, asking questions, or making predictions.

Math Think-Aloud Example

Math example:

63
−27
‾‾‾‾

> Teacher: In this problem, I am subtracting 27 from 63. This means that I have positive 63 and must go to the left on a number line 27.

+60   +3
−20   −7
‾‾‾‾‾‾‾‾

> Teacher: I want to use place value to make better sense of how to do this efficiently. So, I am going to separate the minend, 63, and the sub-trahend, −27, each by their place value and line them up accordingly.

+60   +3
−20   −7
‾‾‾‾‾‾‾‾
+40   −4

> Teacher: I will solve the tens place first and then the ones. 6 tens minus 2 tens is 4 tens. 3 minus 7 on a number line is −4.

+60   +3
−20   −7
‾‾‾‾‾‾‾‾
+40   −4
‾‾‾‾‾‾‾‾
+36

> Teacher: I am left with the two differences per place value as +40 and −4. 40 − 4 is 36. The answer is 36. Looking back over the question of 63 − 27, the answer of 36 makes sense.

A think-aloud is one of the most positive scaffolding strategies you can use. Struggling students need to understand the thought process used in solving problems or reading a text. Without a think-aloud, it's simply a code they don't know how to unlock.

Tool 119
Viewing and Reading Guides

Whether you are asking students to read a type of test or view multimedia, it's important to provide a guide. Otherwise, students won't know what to look for. These can be detailed, or more general. For example, look at the specific prompts in the social studies example below.

Using Guide-O-Ramas

Europe: War and Change—Chapter 12 (Sections 12.1–12.2)

Page	Reading Tip
326	Look at the map. This gives you an idea of where Europe is in relation to the United States.
327	Read the introduction in the yellow box. Can you believe that most Europeans can speak at least three languages? Can you speak any languages other than English?
329–332	Read section 12.1. Pay close attention to the terms nationalism, colonialism, and dual monarchy. They are related and can be confusing!
334–338	As you read this section carefully, make a timeline of which countries joined the war and record the dates when each joined.
335	I found it interesting that dogs were used in the war to detect mines and guard ammunition! Do you think this is humane?
336	Pay close attention to the term fascism. How does this compare to what you know about communism and democracy?

Next, the sample viewing guide is broader, which requires students to narrow down the information from the source.

Broader Viewing Guide

Viewing Guide for _____		
What are the key points in the video?	What examples are given for each of the main points?	What questions do you have?
What is the most important thing you learned from the video?		

Tool 120
Post-it Notes

Post-it or sticky notes can be an effective tool during lessons. My struggling students particularly liked these notes because there is a limited amount of writing required. When I asked them to write on a sheet of paper, many gave up before they started. They were afraid they had to fill up the entire paper.

If students are reading a text, whether in print or electronically, they can use four colors of post it notes. Yellow is for the main idea; blue is for a key word and definition; green is for a question they have, and pink is for an example of the author's perspective.

Speteacher(http://teachers.post-it.com/wps/portal/3M/en_US/Post-it-Teachers/ Home/Featured-Activities/) explains a different way she uses Post-its:

We have a poster board with Brain Flow and a brain (from the dollar tree in the Halloween section). At the end of class the students have to answer the question of the day. It may be what did you learn during 3rd period today, what did you say nice to someone today, or what is your homework tonight. Even the students get to decide the question to ask. The answer is put on a Post-it note for each student and put on the board. The next morning I collect the Post-its and place them in a notebook with the date and what the question was. The students really enjoy seeing who writes what and most of the time they will say "Oh yea, we did learn that today."

Tool 121
Layering Meaning

Layering meaning is also a useful strategy for working with struggling students. If a student cannot read the grade-level or assigned text material, find another text on the same topic that is written at an easier level. Students read that selection first, and build their own prior knowledge and vocabulary, then they can go back and read the more complex text with your support. Since the CCSS discourage teachers' building background for students, this is an excellent way for students to take ownership of the process, rather than you directing or telling them the information.

After Lesson Strategies

After you have taught your lesson, there are additional strategies that are important to support your struggling learners.

Tool 122
Supporting Answers with Evidence

It's important for students to learn to support any conclusions or inferences they make with evidence. This is particularly true with the CCSS, which require that students pull direct evidence from the text or multimedia source. I always told my students that support was like a chair; the conclusion they made was the seat of the chair, and evidence was a leg of a chair. If you only have one or two legs, you don't have a very strong chair. This visual helped them see the importance of backing up their statements with clear and specific examples.

Another visual that is helpful is a grove of trees. Each tree trunk is a conclusion, and the branches are their specific points that support the conclusion. Either of these can help your students follow through on their comments with evidence.

Tool 123
Probing, Extending, and Sustaining Questions

Although we are discussing questions in our after lesson section, you would also want to use questioning throughout your lesson. In addition to your initial question to a student, the follow-up questions that probe, extend, or sustain the discussion are critical.

Examples of Follow-Up Questions

Why do you think that is true?

What are some examples of your point?

How did you come to that conclusion?

Where did you find that information?

If _____ is true, then what might happen next?

That's a great start to the answer. Now, what else do you know about it?

Consider providing an opportunity for students to discuss answers with a partner or in small groups before sharing out with the larger group. This gives time for reflection, and the discussion will help students flesh out their answers before explaining them to the whole class.

Tips for Follow-Up Questions

Plan your questions in advance.

Sketch out possible answers from your students. Be prepared to deal with unexpected responses.

Be sure your questions are clear and understandable.

If you use a Yes/No question, immediately follow it up with a "Why" or "How" question.

If a student doesn't know the answer, ask guiding questions to help them come up with the answer, rather than just moving on.

Be sure you don't answer the question while you are asking it. Leading questions don't require students to understand the content.

Tool 124
Reworking Tests

Kendra Alston, former teacher and now Academic Facilitator at Kennedy Middle School, uses mini-assessments after each test. If you look at Kendra's assessment, she immediately goes over the answers, and students must identify what items they missed and why. This shifts the focus from what they did wrong to what they are learning. It also requires they actually learn the material, rather than simply moving on without revisiting their mistakes.

Mini-Assessment

Name _____

Date of Test _____

Test Title _____

Summarize: What was this passage about?

Identify what you missed and why.

Make a list of what you missed. Place the number that fits beside each item.

1 I didn't understand the question.
2 I thought I had this right.
3 I studied this but forgot.
4 I have no clue about this.
5 I ran out of time and didn't try this.
6 I made a careless mistake.

Question I missed	I chose	Why	Correct answer

Tool 125
Extra Help

No matter how much scaffolding you provide before, during, and after a lesson, some students still need more support. They either need more time, or they need one-on-one instruction. Most teachers I know provide this extra help for students, possibly before or after school. However, there's a small problem with extra help. Too often, the students who need it the most don't take advantage of your offer. This may be due to logistical issues, but far more often, students don't ask for extra help because they don't know they need it.

For example, Ronnie, one of my students, would leave my class at the end of the day sure he understood our lesson. The next day, he came in, homework incomplete, and unable to explain anything we had done the day before. No matter how often I offered to provide help, he turned me down. He said, "I understand it," even when he didn't. He truly didn't know that he didn't understand—and that is a typical problem.

For our neediest students, we need to require extra help—not make it a volunteer experience. I find this needs to be coordinated school-wide during the school day or it simply isn't manageable. In my case, we used our lunchtime for extra help. A teacher could identify a student who needed assistance, and he or she would bring his or her lunch to a study room, and work with a teacher. That may not be your best option, but I would encourage you to work with your administration and other teachers to find a way to provide mandatory extra help for struggling learners.

Differentiation

Differentiated instruction is a popular concept, and I have heard many interpretations of its meaning. For most teachers, it means creating lessons that include different elements to meet the needs of each individual student in a diverse classroom. According to the technical definition, in differentiated instruction, a teacher varies the content (what), process (how), or product (demonstration of learning) of instruction to enhance student understanding.

Tool 126
Differentiating Content

I spoke with teachers in an elementary school about differentiation of content. They had a large percentage of students working above grade level, some on grade level, and the rest were reading below grade level. Fourth grade teachers typically chose one novel for all students to read each month. One teacher explained, "I'm not sure we're really meeting anyone's needs. The books are fun, but they are too hard for a few students, and I think they are probably too easy for a good portion of my students."

The next month, instead of choosing one book, we found four books at varying readability levels on the same topic. Students were then reorganized in groups based on their ability levels to read and discuss the novels. Each teacher met with one of the four groups to facilitate discussions and ensure understanding. Then students returned to their original classrooms, and all teachers led whole-group discussions about Langston Hughes. A key element of this process was that the different books each contained some information the other groups did not read. During the class discussion, the teachers asked questions to elicit specific information from each group.

One of the benefits was that even students in the lowest reading group had specific information to contribute to the discussion, reinforcing everyone's importance to the group. Also, students who could read at a higher level were challenged to do so. Finally, students were placed into new groups, with members having read the different novels, so they could create a final project about Langston Hughes. By using flexible groupings, the teachers were able to meet their students' needs more effectively.

Langston Hughes Book List

Title	Author(s)	Lexile*
Shatter with Words: Langston Hughes	Margo Sorenson	370L
Langston Hughes: Great American Poet	Patricia and Fredrick McKissack	530L
Coming Home: From the Life of Langston Hughes	Floyd Cooper	AD770L
Langston Hughes: Young Black Poet	Montrew Dunham	860L
Langston Hughes: Poet of the Harlem Renaissance	Christine M. Hill	890L
The Political Plays of Langston Hughes	Susan Duffy and Langston Hughes	1210L
The Life of Langston Hughes	Arnold Rampersad	1290L
Langston Hughes: Folk Dramatist in the Protest Tradition, 1921–1943	Joseph McLaren	1450L

*For more information on Lexiles, see Chapter U: Up or Down.

Tool 127
Learning Centers

Learning centers are popular in primary classrooms, but they are appropriate at all levels. In addition to providing differentiation for students, the independent nature of the work helps them take responsibility for their own learning. If your classroom has an appropriate setup, provide learning stations around the room with different activities all related to the same topic.

Christy Matkovich chooses to use folders for learning centers to enhance the small-group activities she utilizes in her classroom:

At each center there are four different folders, with a number (one through four). When it is center time, if a child sits at a one in his or her group, then he or she may choose a center and complete the activity in folder number one at that center. If a child sits at the three spot in his or her group, then during center time, he or she may choose a center and complete the activity in the folder number three at that center. When preparing activities for each center, I make sure that the concept for all four folders is the same. For example, at center number one, everyone may be working on concepts that involve order of operations. However, the level of difficulty varies based on the folder number. Folders one and two are basic activities, and folders three and four are enrichment activities. This arrangement allows me to challenge the higher-level students and do some remediation for the lower level students. Some centers are set up so that ones and fours work together and twos and threes work together. Although my ones and twos are low, I still want to challenge them. Therefore, on challenging activities, I pair them with the higher-performing students so that they can help and support each other.

Tool 128
Contracts

Many teachers use learning contracts for differentiation of instruction. Students are able to choose a certain number of assignments to complete for a particular grade. In your design, you can allow for different intelligences or learning styles.

High School Biology Contract

Topic: Biological Evolution

I _____, agree to complete four of the following tasks by the end of the nine weeks.

1. Read three articles outside of classroom resources on natural selection and write a brief annotated bibliography including how the information from the articles supplements classroom learning.

2. Infer the fate of a particular species whom you know to be heading toward extinction. Create a 5-minute PSA to save this species.

3. Create a compare/contrast chart to compare micro- and macro-evolution.

4. Create a two voices poem using micro- and macro-evolution.

5. Create a RAFT explaining how changes in the environment may result in the appearance of disappearance of particular traits.

6. Create a twitter account and tweet to your classmates and any other followers about natural selection. In a reflection essay, not to exceed two pages, share what you have learned about natural selection.

Tool 129
Tic-Tac-Toe

Another alternative to a learning contract is to use a tic-tac-toe board. Simply develop your learning activities, and students choose the tasks based on creating a tic-tac-toe.

Sample Tic-Tac-Toe Table
Fifth Grade

Using what you know about the legislative system, choose one branch and convince the other two why it is most important.	Create a two voices poem comaparing the United States government to one of the following: Canadian, Central American or Mexican government	Create a graphic organizer using and comparing the branches of United States branches of government.
Complete the web of political and social institutions on page 184 in order to analyze the two types of institutions.	Write a report about government in the United States. In your report, describe at least two ways local, state, and national government are alike and at least two ways they are different. Use specific examples to support your descriptions.	Create your own RAFT in which the topic is the Declaration of Independence.
Read the preamble to the United States' constitution. Explain why this document is important for American citizens, including at least three specific examples from the document.	Describe how a bill becomes a law to someone who just moved to the United States six months ago. Write your description in paragraph form.	Analyze the Federal System of Government using the graphic organizer on page 199.

Tool 130
Options for Assignments

When I assigned a report to my students, they could choose how to present it to our class. Imagine the depth of understanding needed for a student to summarize a book in a two-minute commercial or video blog or the creativity involved in developing a music video to explain content. If they are allowed to choose how they show you they understand the content, many students will invest more time and effort on the task, and they will demonstrate their learning at a higher level.

Kendra Alston, Academic Facilitator at Kennedy Middle School, shared a learning activity she experienced during a high school social studies class. She wasn't excited to study the 1920s and 1930s, but her teacher, Mr. Baldwin told them he was giving a *show me what you know* final exam:

> *He didn't care how you showed it, as long as you showed what you know. Things flashed before my eyes, but I was into theatre. So I researched the vaudeville circuit at time and found Bessie Smith in theatre. She was a blues singer who sang in speakeasies; and I learned about the 20s and 30s through her eyes. On day of the exam, I came in singing, staying in character. He asked questions and I answered based on what Bessie Smith would have said.*

What a wonderful way to demonstrate understanding of a topic.

Tool 131
Differentiated Homework

Christy Matkovich differentiates the content of homework in her math classroom. As you can see from the examples, students receive the same type of homework and the same number of problems. However, students receive work that is customized to their understanding of the fraction concepts.

Differentiated Homework Activity

QUESTION: Why Did the Bee Become Frustrated While Calling His Mom?

Complete each word problem below. Locate your answer in the appropriate box. Place the letter located next to each word problem in the box that contains the correct answer. Put the letters together to form words that answer the riddle above.

GN   Max and his dad went to eat pizza after the high school foot-ball game on Friday. Max ate 1/4 of a pizza and his dad ate 2/3 of a pizza. How much pizza did they eat altogether?

AB   Sandy and her mother bought 1½ yards of fabric to make Sandy's Halloween costume. If they used ½ yard to make a collar for their new puppy, how much fabric was left for Sandy's costume?

AL   Patrick and Brandon are the best three-point shooters on their basketball team. In the last game, Patrick made ½ of the team points and Brand made ¼ of the team points. What fraction of the team points did they make altogether?

ZY   Mr. Jones has two books about skateboards stacked on his desk. One book is 1/6 of an inch. The second book in 1/3 of an inch. How tall is the stack of books?

SI   The girls track team was practicing for the championship meet. Coach Barnes asked the team to run 1/4 of a mile as a warm-up. At the end of practice, they had to run 3/8 of a mile to cool down. What fraction of a mile did they have to run altogether?

UZ   In science class, students had to measure the length of two different lab tables. Both lab tables together were 2¾ meters long. If one lab table was 1½ meters, how long was the second table?

ANSWER: He kept getting:

1	1¼	½	5/8	11/12	¾
___	___	___	___	___	___

QUESTION: Why Did the Bee Become Frustrated While Calling His Mom?

Complete each word problem below. Locate your answer in the appropriate box. Place the letter located next to each word problem in the box that contains the correct answer. Put the letters together to form words that answer the riddle above.

GN   The football team went to eat pizza after the high school football game on Friday. One player ate 2/8 of pizza, another player ate 1/6 of pizza, and the third player ate ¾ of a pizza. If there were 3 pizzas, how much pizza was left for the rest of the team?

AB   Sandy and her mother bought 24/6 yards of fabric to make Sandy's Halloween costume. If they used 2/3 of a yard to make a collar for their new puppy, and 8/7 of a yard to make a baby costume, how much fabric was left for Sandy's costume?

AL   Patrick, Brandon, and Miguel are the best three-point shooters on their basketball team. In the last game, the team scored 108 points. If Patrick scored 2/9 of the points, Brandon score 1/6 of the points, Miguel scored 1/3 of the points. What fraction of the points did the boys score altogether?

ZY   Mr. Jones has four books about skateboards stacked on his desk. The length of the books are 10¼ inches, 113/16 inches, 93/8 inches, and 11¾ inches. How long would the books be if you laid them end to end?

SI   The girls track team was practicing for the championship meet. The girls team had to run a total of 9 miles during the whole practice. If they ran 13/8 miles for warm-up and 23/10 miles for their first drill, how many miles did they have left to run during practice?

UZ   Ms. Steven placed all the science lab table in a row. The row was 25½ meters long. Each table was 17/10 meters long. If Ms. Steven removed three tables from the row of tables, how long would the new row be?

ANSWER: He kept getting:

11/42	429/16	513/40	232/5	15/6	13/8
_____	_____	_____	_____	_____	_____

Special Populations

In this chapter, we've focused on strategies that help all struggling learners. In this section, we'll look at four specific groups.

> Students with Special Needs
> English Language Learners
> Students from Poverty
> Potential Dropouts

Working with Students with Special Needs

Working with students with special needs can present a variety of challenges. However, just because a student is labeled learning disabled or at risk, it does not mean he or she is incapable of learning. Students with learning disabilities have average to above-average intelligence. Therefore, ensuring their success in school is a matter of finding the appropriate teaching strategies and motivation tools, all of which we can control as teachers.

Tool 132
Dealing with Learned Helplessness

Learned helplessness is a process of conditioning in which student seek help from others even when they have mastered information. See if this example sounds familiar:

A student is asked to solve a direct reading-comprehension problem, but he immediately raises his hand. When the teacher comes over, the student says he needs help. So the teacher reads the paragraph to the student and re-explains the question. The student still doesn't answer the question. Next, the teacher re-explains a regularly used comprehension strategy with the student. Finally, the teacher walks through the strategy and may even solve the problem for the student.

While this teacher's approach sounds justifiable, and maybe even familiar, the teacher is reinforcing the student's learned helplessness. This exchange undermines the student's independent ability to solve the problem. Other behaviors that continue a student's learned helplessness include an increased time of completion, lack of academic perseverance, refusal to initiate an attempt, and general off-task behavior. Thus, once a student has begun a run of learned helplessness, expect to see the behaviors repeatedly. In the scenario above, the student must learn to attend to the teacher's group instruction and attempt to solve problems.

Instead of running to the rescue of students who can succeed without us or even refusing to help such students, it is important to find ways to teach students to gain independence in their problem solving. In other words, find out why the student is behaving in a certain way, and plan a response that best builds academic success and independence. One way to help is to teach students how to learn and succeed without instantly making excuses and asking for help by following seven steps.

Steps for Working with Learned Helplessness

Determine if learned helplessness exists.

Explicitly model the preferred academic behavior.

Teach the student a strategy for displaying the preferred academic behavior.

Provide practice for the strategy.

Set a cue to remind the student to initiate the strategy.

Allow the student to succeed.

Facilitate the student's problem-solving strategy.

Source: Blackburn and Witzel, 2013

Tool 133
Modifications and Accommodations

Many times we use the term *modification* interchangeably with *accommodation*. However, they are very different. A modification is a change in the content of curricular standards; an accommodation is a tool to help one reach the standard. Although we discussed accommodations in Chapter Two, Tool 33, here are samples of each, to help with understanding.

Potential Accommodations and Modifications

Potential Accommodations	Potential Modifications
Extra wait time Procedures clarification Minimize classroom distractions Homework reminders and planners Weekly progress report and home checks Increased 1:1 assistance Classroom signals for attention Guided notes Break lengthy assignments into smaller, more manageable pieces with intermediate deadlines	Altered grading procedures Alternative (but related) standard during lesson Different reading assignments Different questions Alternative assessment content and/or expectations Elimination of parts of assignments if they remove a standard Calculator during math fluency assignment Altered grading procedures Alternative but related standard during lesson Different reading assignments if reading is being assessed

Source: Blackburn & Witzel (2013)

Working with English Language Learners

English Language Learners (ELL) also have specific needs. Although all of the learning supports in this chapter, there are two other tools that are particularly helpful.

Tool 134
Use of Visuals

The use of visuals, which can be helpful for all struggling learners, is especially important with English Language Learners. Many teachers use Word Walls, where they post important vocabulary on a wall or bulletin board. I was in an ELL classroom that capitalized on this strategy, but took it to another level. A piece of paper was folded in half, and the word was written on the outside. Lift up the paper, and you would find a graphic representing the word. Just this little change made a huge difference for the ELL students.

Tool 135
Use of Language

It is important to note that our language as teachers is also important. Whenever possible, simplify your instructions and streamline your questions so that a student's native language does not interfere as much. Additionally, especially for those ELLs who are struggling with English, ask questions that require them to complete a thought, rather than generate a new idea. Beginning with this type of question helps them build confidence and a strong base for future learning.

Working with Students from Poverty

It is important when working with students from a poverty background to not make assumptions. Oftentimes, they do not have the background knowledge other students have. For example, my husband and I had a foster son for several months. Prior to his time with us, he had been homeless, and he grew up in poverty. The first time we took him to a restaurant, he didn't know how to use cloth napkins and he was stunned at the concept of leaving a tip.

Tool 136
Acknowledge Their Perspective

When I was teaching, the majority of my students lived in poverty. However, I grew up in a middle class household. I didn't fully understand their circumstances or perspective. For example, when they didn't do their homework, it was often because they didn't have the resources at home. I would have provided the resources, but they didn't tell me. After all, who wants to admit they don't have paper or pencils at home?

It's important to acknowledge that your students who live in poverty are different; they are members of a group that has specific needs. Because they don't have resources at home, they may never have learned how to organize materials. If their parents aren't educated, education may not be reinforced. They may or may not have positive role models in their lives. Recognizing these facets of your students helps you be more empathetic and more willing to help meet their specific needs.

Tool 137
Making Assumptions, Part Two

One may make the assumption that students who come to school with expensive sneakers and clean clothes would also come to school with the appropriate school supplies such as paper and a pencil or pen. Value is placed on different items with students in poverty. It is not that they cannot afford a pencil or paper. It is more important to come to school and appear "normal" and look and act like other students. Parents will invest in clothes and shoes for their children rather than materials for school. Students in poverty may also have the appropriate materials, yet they will not keep up with them because they are of less value (not monetary) than other materials such as clothes and shoes.

Working with Potential Dropouts

Another group of students who need particular support are those who are potential dropouts. Although I hear many primary school teachers say, "I can predict who is going to drop out just based on their attitudes!", we also know we can predict a potential dropout based on their grades as early as fourth grade. If we wait until high school to meet these students' needs, then we are too late.

Tool 138
Perspectives of Dropouts

The Silent Epidemic: Perspectives of High School Dropouts (Bridgeland et al., 2006) paints an unexpected picture of high school dropouts. Through responses of focus groups and interviews with almost 500 dropouts, we discover that most of these students (88 percent) were not failing school, and 70 percent believed they could have graduated. So what went wrong?

Rigor-Related Findings From The Silent Epidemic
47 percent of dropouts said classes weren't interesting.
43 percent had missed too many days of school and couldn't catch up.
69 percent were not motivated to work hard.
66 percent would have worked harder if more had been demanded of them.

The same students had strong views on what schools should do to help students stay in school. Their recommendations paint a picture of what we can do to meet these students' needs.

Rigor-Related Recommendations From Dropouts

71 percent recommended making school interesting.

55 percent said there should be help for students who have trouble learning.

81 percent called for more "real-world" learning opportunities.

75 percent wanted smaller classes with more individual instruction.

Tool 139
Instant Credit Recovery

The use of a "Not Yet" or "Incomplete" policy for projects and assignments shifts the emphasis to learning and allows students to revise and resubmit work until it is at an acceptable level. Requiring quality work, work that meets the teachers' expectations, lets students know that the priority is learning, not simple completion of an assignment. You'll find more about ICR in Chapter Six.

As part of their comprehensive school reform model, SREB has long been a proponent of holding students to high expectations for completed work. Toni Eubank describes the model as Instant Credit Recovery (or Instant Content Recovery for middle school students):

This grading intervention practice requires that teachers rethink credit recovery completely. If it is okay for students to retake courses to meet standards, why is it not okay to retake tests that do not meet standards, revise essays, redo classwork and homework that do not meet standards? Why do we let students "off the hook" for learning and for completing work that meets the standards during our classes, and then spend thousands and thousands of dollars requiring them to retake entire courses they have failed, many simply because they did not do homework? Instead of sitting in classes throughout the semester or year putting forth little to no effort, doing little work, failing tests or turning in garbage instead of high-quality work, students must now be required to work as they go. This method truly reflects job-embedded skills and habits and better prepares students for college and careers. Instead of retaking courses and earning credit (often for seat time only) in our current credit recovery programs, students must now work while they go—sort of a "pay as you go" method (Eubank, 2011, p. 1).

Instant Credit Recovery is particularly helpful for those students who cannot see a reason to stay in school, due to their unsuccessful classwork. It's motivating, and it keeps students on track for graduation.

Conclusion

As students move to higher levels of rigor, they need additional support and scaffolding to be successful. There is a variety of effective strategies that should occur before, during, and after a lesson. Additionally, specific strategies can help our special populations. The challenge is to determine the right tool for the right student at the right time.

Reflection into Action

1. What are three main tools from this chapter you could use in your classroom?

2. Which of those three will you put into place in the next three days?

3. Are there any resources you need to make this happen?

4. Which one would you like to implement next week?

5. What other tools do you want to consider for the future?

6. Is there anything else from this chapter you want to remember after you finish the book?

6
Options for Assessment

In this chapter, we'll discuss facets of assessment in a rigorous classroom. Although summative assessments in the form of standardized testing are important, we'll leave that topic for another book. Instead, we'll look at five main topics.

> Formative Assessment
> Quality Assignments
> Feedback
> Homework
> Grading

Formative Assessment

Formative assessment is one of the hottest buzzwords in education today. A Google search nets over a quarter of a million hits! I strongly believe that if we are going to truly support our students to higher levels, we must continually assess their learning and use that information to plan our future instruction. In 1998, Black and Wiliam provided a clear rationale that using formative assessment effectively raises standards. In 2004, they and other researchers provided a fuller explanation of formative assessment in *Working Inside the Black Box: Assessment for Learning in the Classroom.*

Assessment for learning is any assessment for which the first priority in its design and practice is to serve the purpose of promoting pupils' learning. It thus differs from assessment designed primarily to serve the purposes of accountability or of ranking or of certifying competence. An assessment activity can help learning if it provides information to be used as feedback, by teachers, and by their pupils, in assessing themselves and each other, to modify the teaching and learning activities in which they are engaged (Black et al., 2004).

What does that mean to you as you consider your current assessments, whether they are tests, projects, homework, or a mix of items? Let's back up for a minute.

131

Many assessments used in classrooms are summative. In other words, they are used to evaluate a student. We will discuss that more in terms of grading later in this chapter. However, formative assessments are used to help a student and teacher adjust to improve learning.

Tool 140
Characteristics of Formative Assessment

In *Advancing Formative Assessment in Every Classroom: A Guide For Instructional Leaders*, Brookhart and Moss describe the characteristics of formative assessment.

Characteristics of Formative Assessment

Formative Assessment (Assessment *for* Learning)
Purpose: To improve learning and achievement
Carried out while learning is in progress.
Focused on the learning process and progress.
Viewed as an integral part of the teaching-learning process.
Collaborative—Teachers and students know where they are headed, understand the learning needs, and use assessment information as feedback to guide and adapt what they do to meet those needs.
Fluid—An ongoing process influenced by student need and teacher feedback.
Teachers and students adopt the role of intentional learners.
Teachers and students use the evidence they gather to make adjustments for continuous improvement.

Tool 141
Transformative Assessment

James Popham (2008) notes that true formative assessment is actually transformative. He describes four levels of implementation.

Let's take a look at Level 3 of Popham's transformative assessment, which "represents a complete change in the culture of a classroom, shifting the overriding role of classroom assessment from the means to compare students with one another for grade assignments to the means to generate evidence from which teachers and students can, if warranted, adjust what they're doing" (p. ix).

Level Three of Popham's Transformative Assessment

Area	From	To
Learning Expectations	Substantial learning will occur for motivated students who possess adequate academic aptitude.	Substantial learning will occur for all students, irrespective of their academic aptitude
Responsibility for Learning	The teacher, as prime instructional mover, is chiefly responsible for students' learning.	Students assume meaningful responsibility for their own learning and the learning of their classmates.
Role of Classroom Assessment	Formal tests generate data for comparing students and assigning grades.	Formal and informal assessments generate data for informing adjustments to the teacher's instruction and the students' learning tactics.

Source: Popham, 2008, p. 95

Teacher-Directed Formative Assessment

There is a variety of ways you can direct formative assessment throughout the lesson. In fact, all of the activities described in Chapters Four and Five can be used as formative assessment if you pay attention to how students are learning, and make adjustments based on what you see. But there are several other methods you can use.

Tool 142
Demonstrating Understanding Through Four Corners

Four Corners is an excellent way to work through multiple-choice questions. After discussing the question, students choose their answer by going to one of the corners of your room. Then, ask students to discuss their answers in the small groups. Next, share out to the large group and give students an opportunity to change their selection. It's a visible way to see students' understanding and allow for immediate feedback on learning.

Tool 143
Demonstrating Understanding Through Pair/Shares

Another way to use formative assessment is through pair/share or think/pair/share. Periodically, ask students to stop, turn to a partner, and answer a question. This allows each student to think about the content, and to discuss an answer. Then, you can ask a couple of pairs to share their response. Additionally, a simple way to make this more rigorous is to ask a student to share their partner's response with the whole group, rather than sharing their own. This requires students to listen at a higher level during the pair/share, as well as understanding the partner's answer well enough to share it with the group. Pair/share allows you to monitor students' understanding of the lesson at points throughout the lesson, ensuring comprehension.

Students' Reflections

A different type of formative assessment is student reflections. In this case, students think about their own learning, and provide feedback to the teacher about what they think they know and don't know. We discussed entrance and exit slips in Chapter Four, which are an excellent example of this concept. However, they may also reflect on how they are learning, or their confidence level about understanding the content. Let's look at examples of both.

Reflecting on What I Know

There are many informal ways to have students reflect on what they have learned. You can do this orally by simply asking questions, or you can ask students to create an internet ad, selling what they learned today in your class. The reflections don't have to be long, nor do they need to be extensive.

Tool 144
1-2-3 Times Two

In this activity, students make observations, conclusions, and create questions, but they must back each one up with support from the discussion or text.

One-Two-Three Process

One	Two	Three
One observation	One conclusion	One question
Two examples or supporting comments	Two specific text statements to support	Two prompting phrases

Tool 145
"I" Responses

You can use these prompts throughout the lesson. Students are asked to finish the prompts below to discuss their learning.

> **"I" Response Prompts**
>
> I learned . . .
>
> I think . . .
>
> I was surprised when . . .
>
> I didn't understand . . .
>
> I discovered . . .
>
> I told my partner that . . .
>
> I figured out . . .

Tool 146
CROWN

A more formal form of an exit slip, students respond to a variety of items to show they understand the content.

> **CROWN**
>
> **C**ommunicate what you learned
>
> **R**eact to what you learned
>
> **O**ne sentence summary
>
> **W**ay(s) to use what you learned
>
> **N**ote how well you did today

Tool 147
Learning Logs

I've also seen teachers use journals effectively. Students write entries explaining the main idea they learned in the lesson and a question they still have. These serve as a springboard for review or discussion during the next class. Or the journal can be used as a learning log. Every day at the end of class, students write down at least one thing they learned. By the end of the week, they have a list of at least five things they have learned, by the end of the month they have 20, and so on. This is more authentic than a test and allows students to see and personalize what they are learning.

Reflecting on How I'm Learning

You also may want students to think about how they learn. In other words, you want them to develop metacognitive skills—thinking about their own thinking.

Tool 148
Reworking Tests

Math teachers Lindsay Grant and Christy Matkovich incorporate opportunities in which students can reflect on their own learning processes. Students are given the opportunity to rework any problems that were incorrect on a test. As the graphic organizer shows, students are also asked to think about their learning by explaining why they missed the original question and why they know they have the correct answer now. As Lindsay explains, the process "makes them think about what they've done and what they did differently or what they are supposed to do."

Understanding Math Better

Name _____   Date _____

Math Test _____   Teacher _____

Question:

My Original Answer:

My New Solution (you must show your work including all steps):

The Correct Answer:

Why I Missed the Question on the Original Test (circle one):

    I didn't understand the question.

    I thought I had it right.

    I skipped a step.

    I studied this but I forgot.

    I had no clue about this.

    I ran out of time or guessed.

    I made a careless mistake.

Why I Know I Have the Right Answer Now:

Tool 149
Laundry Day

In laundry day, students group themselves in four categories. With the groupings, you can then determine how much reteaching needs to occur.

Laundry Day

Category	Student's Perspective
Tide	I'm drowning in information.
Gain	I understand the basics, but I'm missing a few parts.
Bold	I'm confident, but I'm missing some details.
Cheer	I'm sure I understand, so I'm looking for something new.

Tool 150
Other Options for Formative Assessment

Other Formative Assessment Options

Individual White Boards

Clickers for Computer Summary of Data

Apps such as Show Me for the iPad

Graphic Organizers

Monitoring of Conversations

Observations

Short Quizzes

Quality Assignments

There are three aspects of quality assignments: whether or not the assignment is appropriate, whether it is purposeful, and whether it is results-oriented.

Tool 151
Assignment is Appropriate

First, assignments should be appropriate. What do I mean by that? I mean they should be at a rigorous level. Too often, we water our assignments down to make them easier for students. For example, I was in a first grade classroom where students were working on numbers up to ten. The assignment was to simply color ten crayons in various groupings, despite the fact that was too easy, based on the earlier work. In another class, the teacher was using a much higher assessment that was more rigorous and required students to use higher order thinking.

Solve the problem. Show your work.
I have 10 crayons. Some are red. Some are blue. How many of each could I have? How many red? How many blue?
Find as many combinations as you can.

Tool 152
Bloom's Taxonomy Questions

Your questions should also be at an appropriate level of rigor. We discussed Bloom's Taxonomy in Chapter Three: Raise Expectations through Questioning and Adult Behaviors, but let's look again at some questions that would be at differing levels. In each of the examples, you would want to use the questions or prompts at the highest level possible. You may need to use the lower levels as a base, but it's important to move up the levels.

Sample Bloom's Taxonomy Questions

HOTS for *Lord of the Flies* by William Golding (novel)

Bloom's Revised	Questions for Literature
Creating	Imagine that you are one of the survivors from the island rescued by the British Naval Officer, upon returning home, you face an angry mob of parents. You learn that the survivors will attend a court hearing for the deaths of Piggy and Simon. Build a case justifying who is guilty of the murders of Piggy and Simon.
Evaluating	How is *Lord of the Flies* an allegory for World War II?
Analyzing	Explain who is a better leader, Jack or Ralph?
Applying	What does the conch symbolize?
Understanding	What happened in chapter 2?
Remembering	Who is the fair hair boy?

HOTS for *Cask of Amontillado* by Edgar Allan Poe (short story)

Bloom's Revised	Questions for Literature
Creating	Imagine this story told from the point of view of Fortunato. Create his story and remember to include his reactions, feelings, escape, and attempts of trying to understand Montressor.

see next page

Bloom's Revised	Questions for Literature
Evaluating	Why do you think Fortunato becomes silent at the end except for the bells on his fool's hat?
Analyzing	Why is Montressor considered an unreliable narrator?
Applying	How is Montressor's situation similar to General Zaroff's from "The Most Dangerous Game"?
Understanding	Write a summary of the story in twenty words or less.
Remembering	What is the Montressor family motto?

HOTS for "Free At Last" by Martin Luther King, Jr. (speech—primary source for social studies)

Bloom's Revised	Questions for Literature
Creating	Create your own speech using "Free At Last" as inspiration to save the oppressed from the injustice of big government.
Evaluating	Why does Martin Luther King use words that compare the rights of American citizens to a check?
Analyzing	Compare Abraham Lincoln's "Gettysburg Address" to Martin Luther King, Jr.'s "Free At Last."
Applying	Show how historical events prior to August 28, 1963 inspired Martin Luther King's speech "Free At Last."
Understanding	Paraphrase Martin Luther King's speech in your own words.
Remembering	What does it mean to be free?

HOTS for "Electric Light Bulbs Toys With Our Internal Clocks" by Joel Shurkin (Science Article) www.livescience.com/38619-electric-light-bulbs-toy-with-our-internal-clocks.html (accessed 08/12/13)

Bloom's Revised	Questions for Literature
Creating	Hypothesize other variables that may account for different effects on subject sleeping patterns other than light.
Evaluating	Determine if Thomas Edison's invention of the light bulb is responsible for people's lack of sleep in today's world.
Analyzing	Compare the amount of lumens given off by incandescent light bulbs and sunlight. Explain how the amount of lumens affects melatonin levels in humans.
Applying	How did the scientists use sound scientific practices?

see next page

Bloom's Revised	Questions for Literature
Understanding	What was the study about in this article?
Remembering	Which hormone is responsible for sleeping?

HOTS for "12 Tech Trends Transforming Careers—And Leading To New Jobs" by Daniel Burrus (Career/Tech Article) http://jobs.aol.com/articles/2013/03/20/technology-career-trends-opportunities/

Bloom's Revised	Questions for Literature
Creating	Design the career requirements for your dream job when you graduate from high school that you would pitch to a company so they would hire you.
Evaluating	Are Burrus' forecasts for the future of technology in careers accurate?
Analyzing	Investigate how businesses already use social media as a marketing tool.
Applying	How has your life as a student changed since you started school in Kindergarten?
Understanding	What are the keys to getting ahead of the curve?
Remembering	According to the article, what are the three change accelerators?

Tool 153
Assignment is Purposeful

Next, the assignment should be purposeful. Rather than giving work simply to give work is not appropriate. When I was teaching, a fellow teacher gave homework every night—no matter what. Much of the work was busy work, but she felt that she should give them something to do every night, regardless of whether the work was needed.

As you think about in-class and out-of-class assignments, consider the standard(s) you are teaching, the type of thinking you want to see from students, and the ultimate product you would like. For example, you may want to prepare students for a multiple-choice test. If so, some of your questions should be multiple-choice. However, the questions should include applications and thinking questions, rather than just guessing questions about basic facts.

In Angie Wiggins' sixth-grade social studies classroom, she was teaching about ancient cultures. She also incorporates rigorous work, and wanted her students to work over time to do research. She designed an assignment that students worked on both in class and outside of class. You'll find the assignment is easily adaptable to other grade levels.

> *Choose a culture and a topic that you are interested in and that relates to one of the ancient cultures in the sixth grade social studies curriculum. Decide on your research questions that are broad and will provide interesting information. Complete your research, using at least three sources. Take notes during your research. Create a museum exhibit about your culture and topic. Present your research in a costume that will represent your culture's clothing. Bring and serve a food that would have been eaten by the people of your culture.*

Tool 154
Assignment Yields Results

Finally, your assignment should yield quality results. In one of his high school classes, my son was given a list of 250 words to memorize for a class. The words would be used throughout the year. Rather than simply memorizing them, it would be more appropriate to introduce the words in context when they are relevant to the content. Then they could be part of the lesson, with a focus not only on the definition but also on the related concepts and possible examples and non-examples. This allows for full comprehension rather than simple memorization. Which result do you prefer?

In a different class, he was given a far more rigorous project. Notice the high level of thinking that is required in a social studies assignment on ancient Greece.

> *Study the image in the site. Imagine that you are a member of the Sir Arthur Evans' archaeological team excavating the palace of Knossos. Write an entry in your archaeology notebook for each of the following artifacts: the fresco of the leaping bull, the fresco of the three women in blue, and the Queen's Hall fresco. In your entries, write about what each artifact reveals about the social, religious, and artistic aspects of the Minoan civilization.*

Last, let's compare two different assignments for third grade math. The first question was to use a graph to identify data. Although a good starting point, it needs to lead to more rigorous work. The teacher scaffolded the work, then in the final problem, students were required to collect, organize, record, and display data in pictographs and bar graphs where each picture or cell might represent more than one piece of data. Interpret the data. What a great example of a quality assignment.

Feedback

Feedback is a critical aspect of assessment, whether formal or informal. It doesn't matter if you are providing feedback orally or in written form, it is a crucial part of students improving their work.

Tool 155
Characteristics of Effective Feedback

Douglas Reeves, in Elements of Grading, describes four characteristics of feedback.

Four Characteristics of Feedback

Characteristic	Description
Accuracy	Should be accurate in terms of content. Asks for accurate answer(s). Based on actual work from student.
Fairness	Be careful not to let expectations about who the student is affect grading or assessment. Focus on the work, not the personality.
Specific	If there is flexibility in the criteria, there should be clear boundaries that students understand.
Timely	If you want students to improve, the feedback should be timely, otherwise, it delays the lesson impact.

Tool 156
Feedback Process

Feedback is a process, one that should become an impetus for growth by students. John Hattie provides a visual that helps us understand the nature of feedback (p. 143).

Tool 157
Teacher Feedback During Questioning

When I taught, one of my challenges was providing feedback during questioning. During a group discussion, if a student answered correctly, I knew to say, "That's exactly on point." Or "That's a great response that hits the nail on the head." But when a student was incorrect or only partially answered the question, I was stuck. What do you say then? On page 144, you'll find a feedback chart that describes how to handle each of those situations. By the way, it's a great handout to leave for a substitute teacher, so they will know what to do.

Hattie Model of Feedback

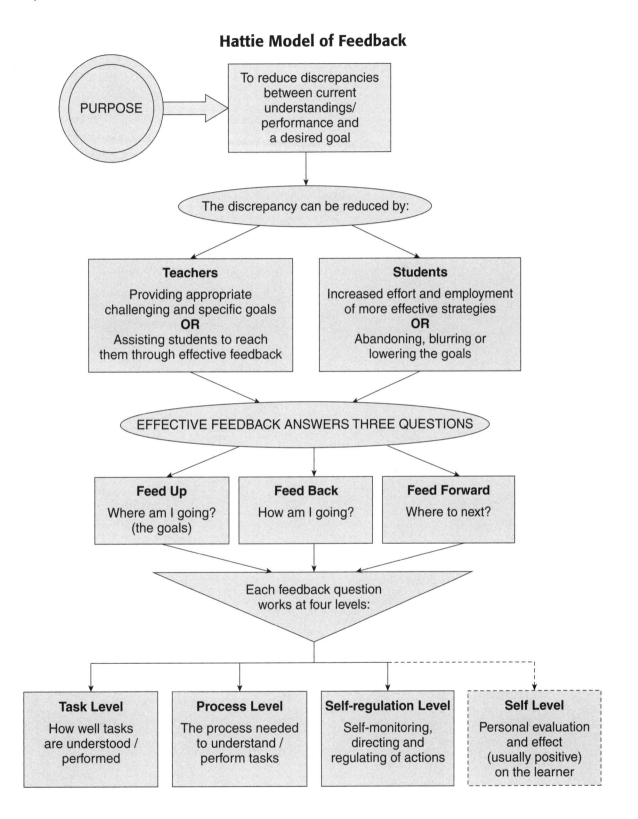

Teacher Feedback Chart

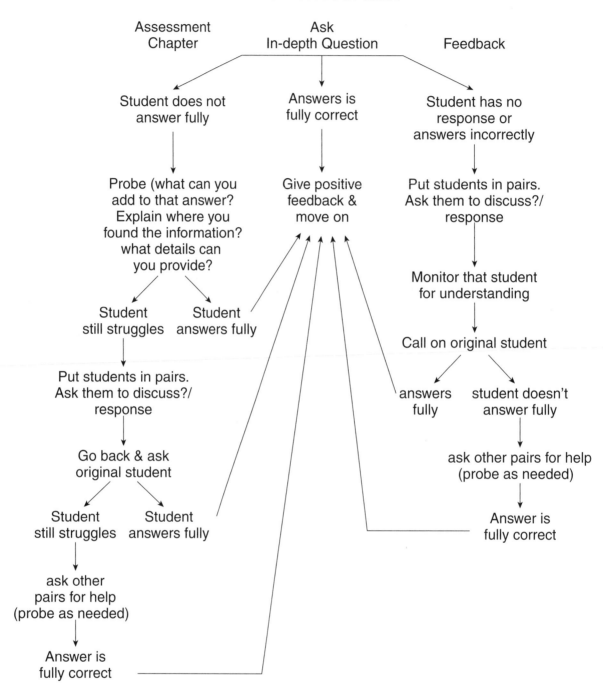

Tool 158
1-2-3

Brenda Martin believes students need to be explicitly taught how to give and receive feedback. She uses a three-step approach, both for her own feedback and for feedback students give each other.

> 1. Begin with a genuine, specific compliment.
> 2. Ask a question to encourage improvement (a question is less threatening and allows the writer to make a decision about the improvement).
> 3. End with an encouraging statement: "You can do it."

Dani Sullivan agrees, explaining, "When grading papers I write more than 'great job' or mark a failing grade. I leave specific comments that are encouraging, ask a question about their work, or select something specific they did well, 'I really like how you shared your logic in your marginal notes. It is clear that you understand the topic of this article.'"

Both teachers provide excellent models that we can follow to provide feedback to our students.

Homework

Homework is an issue for many students and teachers. In almost every workshop that I do on classroom motivation, a teacher will ask, "How do you motivate students to do homework?" Of course, the answer is complicated. You can make students do homework by increasing rewards or punishment, but that rarely works in the long term. The real solution is to create homework assignments that students are most likely to complete and then provide the support necessary to help them be successful. Effective homework is based on three key principles.

> **Three Principles of Effective Homework**
> Purpose-driven
> Quality-driven
> Student-driven

Three Principles of Effective Homework

Tool 159
Purpose-Driven Homework

Homework should have a clear purpose, and students should understand the purpose of the assignment or activity. During my first year of teaching, another teacher told me to assign homework every night. I didn't realize that by following her advice, I was teaching my students that homework is an item to check off a list, not something of authentic value. Homework is an extension of your instruction, so it should always have a specific purpose, just like your lessons. As Shannon Knowles, a sixth-grade teacher says, "Explaining why I'm assigning the homework helps to get it done; I don't give homework just to give homework."

Effective homework assignments extend, reinforce, or preview content. If students have mastered the material, you may choose to assign an independent project to enhance their understanding or allow them to apply their knowledge. After a unit on creating spreadsheets, you might ask students to build a budget using a spreadsheet. However, if students are just beginning to understand a skill, you may want them to complete additional practice to reinforce the knowledge. When I taught parts of speech, for example, I would ask students to find examples from real life (internet articles, newspapers, etc.) and bring them to class. At times, my homework previewed upcoming content. For example, one day, I asked my students to make a list of places that they or their family had visited. The next day, when we discussed the regions of the state, we plotted their vacation sites on the map and categorized them by region.

Tool 160
Quality-Driven Homework

Homework is more effective when the focus is on quality as opposed to quantity. More is not necessarily better, particularly when students are just beginning to understand a concept. I once heard a speaker say, "Practice doesn't make perfect. Perfect practice makes perfect." That made me think about homework. If students don't understand how to do something but practice it 50 times, they will learn the wrong thing. I would prefer to give my students small opportunities to show me they understand so that I can build on that foundation in the future.

In addition to considering quality over quantity, we must consider the homework itself. Quality includes higher order thinking, applications, or pulling together information for use in an advanced activity. For example, one assignment I reviewed included the following items.

Sample Homework Assignment

Homework to Assign:
► After reviewing information in their logbooks, students are to write a forecast for next week's weather. An explanation is to accompany the forecast.
► Students are to continue to record anecdotal information about the weather in their personal weather logbooks. Encourage them to add new weather symbols to their notes.

OPTIONAL SUPPLEMENTAL ACTIVITIES
• Provide a worksheet about reading weather maps.
• Provide a concept review worksheet that matches definitions with vocabulary words from the last six lessons.
• Have students review their vocabulary words and make a crossword or wordfind puzzle.
• Have students add information from this lesson to their weather science notebooks, including:
    - the key features of weather maps,
    - the advantages and disadvantages of using measurement to forecast weather,
    - the advantages and disadvantages of using one's own personal observations to forecast weather,
    - a definition of the word "microclimates".
• Use data from the class weather chart to calculate average, graph information and reveal data patterns.
• Use the calculated data to make graphs and analyse the results.
• Use simple spread sheets to calculate averages, graph information and reveal data patterns.
• Work with the class to compare the accuracy of the local media's weather forecasts with what the class predicts.
• Continue from the rest of the year to have students report local weather data to the class and/or the school.

Source: www.discoverysciencelearning.com/weather_zone/weather_lesson _extras.html

Some of the items, such as creating a forecast from their logbooks with an accompanying explanation are excellent. It uses higher order thinking and requires them to justify their prediction. However, in the supplemental activities there is an activity that would not be considered rigorous; matching vocabulary words with definitions.

Analysis of Homework Assignment

Quality Items	Items to be Improved
Forecasting Weather	Worksheet about Weather (dependent on quality)
Logging weather to use in long-term assignment	Matching Vocabulary
Creating word puzzle	Add basic information to notebooks
Using data for math applications	(should be done in class)

Tool 161
Student-Driven Homework

Homework should provide students an opportunity to be successful. On one occasion, I was in an elementary school classroom watching a lesson on fractions. I'm not sure who was more frustrated—the teacher or the students. As the students became more confused, the teacher finally stopped and said, "This isn't working. Do the rest for homework." The students had absolutely no idea how to proceed, and their likelihood of success was minimal. As Christy Matkovich, a math teacher, points out, "If the day doesn't go well, if students are lost and confused, I just scratch through the lesson and we start over the next day. If I send home practice after a day like that, they'll create a way to do it, then have to unlearn what they did wrong." Don't waste your time or your students' efforts on work that offers no opportunity for success.

Effective homework can be completed independently with minimal and appropriate support. If the assignment is too difficult, students are more likely to ask someone else to complete it for them. When I taught, I tried to create homework assignments that allowed for family members to be involved, but in an appropriate way. For example, I would ask students to write a paragraph and then ask someone else to read it and tell them whether they had clearly stated the main idea. Or, students would interview a family member or a friend about a topic, and we used the responses in our lessons to provide context or build background.

Finally, students should feel ownership about the homework. In some cases, it's appropriate to ask students to help develop the homework. I visited a high school class in which the teacher did exactly that. The students brainstormed appropriate options, then agreed upon the one activity they would all do that night. Another option is to create a BINGO board with choices of activities. Students choose the activities to create a winning board.

Tool 162
Sample Homework Activities

Let's look at some other sample homework activities. For middle school language arts, you could use the following essay questions to follow a reading or discussion.

Why do you think Mark Twain wanted to use a pen name rather than his real name? Come up with a pen name for yourself. Explain what it means to you and why you chose it.

Imagine growing up with very little money, just like Mark Twain. How would you handle the situation? Write a short story about the experiences you might have and the people you might meet along the way.

Source: www.education.com/files/268101_268200/268134/mark-twain-house.pdf

Or in a high school social studies class, after lessons on the Vietnam War, students might write an essay arguing for or against the Vietnam Memorial in Washington, DC.

One of my favorite homework activities comes from an elementary school teacher. She wanted to encourage independent reading with her first graders, so she created reading kits. She found several plastic lunch boxes and transformed each one into a reading project. Inside each box, she placed a book and an activity card. If any supplies were needed (including paper, crayons, or a pencil), she included them in the box. Students were able to take the lunch box home over the weekend to read the book and complete the activity. As she explains, "I never had a problem getting the materials back. My students loved taking the boxes home; they saw it as a treat. And they always completed the activities."

Another teacher in one of my workshops said that she asked her students to bring to class a list or digital picture of ten items found in their kitchen at home. Along with the list, students wrote the size of the item and whether it was a quart, a gallon, 16 ounces, a pound, etc. She used this as a springboard for a unit on measurement.

Kendra Alston uses interactive homework:

I'll take a picture of something my students did in school. Then, I write 'Ask me what I learned today' at the top of the page. The parents have to write what their son or daughter said. This lets me know if the students even remember what happened. I'm also always about getting feedback on my own performance and when the parent writes a reflection on what their child is learning, it gives you insight on how well you taught." This type of homework requires students to understand what they did in class well enough to explain it to someone else—a high standard. One student told me that she liked this assignment because "it's homework for my mom, not me!"

Grading

Grading is one of the most challenging aspects of a rigorous classroom. Many of the aspects of grading, such as whether to grade homework, are individual choices for a teacher. A key consideration for grading is your purpose.

Tool 163
Purposes of Grading

What is your purpose for grading a particular assignment? Are you setting a benchmark to see which of your students have met a standard? Or are you evaluating their progress, so you can make decisions about your future instruction? One of my problems the first year of teaching was that I didn't have a good answer to that question. In fact, if you asked me why I was grading something, my answer would have been, "So I can have enough grades for the report card."

There are several purposes of evaluation. Schools use evaluation to make decisions about placements, particularly in ability leveled classes or promotion to the next grade level. The process of moving students to higher levels requires some type of evaluative judgment. Teachers also use evaluative data to group students and plan for instruction tailored to specific needs. This is one of the most important uses of evaluation. If you collect information about a student, but don't use it to plan what to teach next (or what to reteach), what use is it? Closely linked to this purpose is the notion of using evaluative data to provide feedback to students, so they can improve. Both purposes require that you plan the type of assessment used to ensure you gain the specific information you need to make decisions.

A final use of grades is to externally motivate students. Some students respond well to this form of motivation; grades are just a higher-stakes version of receiving a pizza for reading books. You simply can't get away from the fact that grades provide external pressure on students. Some thrive in this situation; others suffer. Parents and/or family members may complicate the situation if they value the grades differently or more than the student. No matter your purpose, an overemphasis on grades will undermine learning. Let's take a look at key indicators of effective grading.

How to GRADE

Give Students an Opportunity to Participate in Grading

Remove Effort, Behavior, and Attendance from Grading

Align Grading to Assessment

Don't Give Zeroes

Extra Credit Undermines Authentic Grading

Tool 164
Give Students an Opportunity to Participate in Grading

Students feel more ownership when they have a part. So, involve them in the grading process. Be sure they understand what the grade represents, have them look at samples and grade the items themselves, ask them to self-assess their work, and let them create rubrics. In one classroom, the students determined the levels for rubrics.

As the teacher explained, "I didn't particularly like the names for some of the levels, but the students chose them, so I stayed with them."

Student-Created Categories

4 . . . overachiever

3 . . . proficient-got it

2 . . . stuck in the middle

1 . . . at the bottom

After students create the levels, guide them through the process of what would be an "A" or "B," etc. Student ownership doesn't mean you aren't involved; it simply means you guide the process rather than doing it all yourself. After the rubric is finished, ask students to assess a sample paper so they see how the rubric applies to actual work. Then, revise it together, and you can move forward with its use. It's an excellent way for students to be invested in grading.

Tool 165
Remove Effort, Behavior, and Attendance from Grading

One of the mistakes I made as a teacher was grading on things that didn't involve the actual work. For example, if a student "tried hard," I gave them credit for their effort. So as long as they attempted to do the work, the student received partial credit, whether any of it was correct. I've since learned to give students multiple opportunities to complete the work correctly, along with coaching the student, but effort alone does not qualify for a high grade.

Next, I unconsciously graded based on behavior. It wasn't that blatant, of course, but if I had a student who was well behaved, and there was a questionable call on the grade, I gave the student the benefit of the doubt. I should have graded equally, no matter what a student's behavior was. But I was young, and didn't realize I was doing it.

Finally, it's easy to incorporate attendance into grading. If a student was absent, I'd take points off for each day they were late with the assignment. It didn't matter why they were absent; my policy demanded points taken off for late work. In effect, I penalized students because they weren't at school. Some had good reasons for missing, some less so. But the bottom line was that I was choosing to grade, not on their work, but on their presence.

If I could return to my classroom and do it again, I would remove these three factors from grading. A grade should reflect the quality of work, not anything else.

Tool 166
Align Grading to Assessment

It's important to align your grading to the actual assessment. That may sound basic, but I've often seen an assignment that called for certain outcomes, but the grade was based on other criteria. How frustrating for a student. Rubrics are an excellent tool to help you align grading to the assignment. Start by looking at the assignment, develop categories of the criteria, then write the qualities for each category for each grade.

Rubric for Civil War Song

	Excellent 9–10 points	Average 7–8 points	Weak 5–6 points
Song Analysis	A typed report thoroughly analyzes the song lyrics and provides information about the background of the song. (one page minimum—size 12 font). It is well organized, and spelling/grammar mistakes are minimal.	The report gives basic information about the song but does not thoroughly analyze it (as outlined in the project description). The report may be unorganized and difficult to follow.	The report presents minimal information about the song. No analysis is included (only one paragraph).
	Excellent 9–10 points	**Average 7–8 points**	**Weak 5–6 points**
Presentation	Your presentation is well-rehearsed. The typed lyrics to the song are provided and shown via the document camera, and the actual song is played/sung for classmates.	You have neglected to provide either the lyrics or the actual song; your presentation would have benefited from more rehearsal.	You have neglected to provide either the lyrics or the song; your presentation was confusing and did not teach your peers anything about Civil War period music.
Civil War Song Chart	An attractive chart with an extensive list of Civil War songs you have listened to is provided along with brief information about the lyrics.	The chart provided is lacking in song quantity, lyric summary, or neatness.	You have not utilized the song chart to help you learn about Civil War music (very few songs and missing summaries).

Sample Project for 10th Grade Honors Course

History Projects #1 _____ Due: (one week) _____

Wanted Poster

We have studied individuals who made significant contributions during the Renaissance and Reformation. You will create a wanted poster about one of these people. The information on the poster must include:

1. Poster **MUST** be on an 8½ × 11 sheet of paper. **(10 points)**
2. Mug shot—We need to know what they look like! **(10 points)**
3. First and Last name of your historical figure. **(5 points)**
4. Birth Date and Year of Death. **(5 points)**
5. What country were they born in **and** where did they do their work? **(10 points)**
6. What are they famous (wanted) for? 5–8 complete sentences, in your own words, for full credit. **(30 points)**
7. A fact that you found interesting **OR** a quote by the person. **(10 points)**
8. Print out or photocopy of your sources with info highlighted. **(15 points)**
9. Your name on the bottom right corner. **(5 points)**

Revised Grading Guidelines

Percentage of Grade	Requirements
20%	Connections: narrative includes key life events, family, possible associates, other locations visited or other places the person lived to help with locating person.
25%	Synthesis based on multiple sources (minimum of 5): information in paper is synthesized and confirmed from multiple sources, rather than summarized from an isolated source. It is also cited appropriately to demonstrate synthesis.
25%	Analysis: as a conclusion, narrative includes an analysis of the individual, including strengths, weaknesses, and possible other contributions the person could have made to the movement. Although your opinion, analysis should be based on the information gathered.
20%	Written narrative: overall flow and quality of writing, appropriate information included, extraneous information excluded. Quotes and other information support key points made throughout the paper.
10%	Basic requirements: completion of all aspects of assignment, 8"×10" paper, "mug shot," your name at bottom right corner, reference list in appropriate format on reference page, word-processed narrative with 12-point font and 1-inch margins, minimum of 5 sources, and photocopy of sources with information highlighted.

Also, be sure that your grade reflects the quality of the work, not just completion or the quantity of included items. I received a copy of an assignment for a tenth-grade honors course. Students had a week to complete the project. Take a look.

There are several ways to increase the rigor of this assignment. Rather than earning credit for completion, as it is now, scoring should be based on quality.

Tool 167
Don't Give Zeroes

Too often, students don't complete work that requires a demonstration of learning. Typically, this results in a low grade. We often think this means students learn the importance of responsibility, but more often they learn that if they are willing to "take a lower grade or a zero," then they do not actually have to complete their work. For some, that is a preferable alternative to doing work. Perhaps they don't fully understand the assignment or they may not want to complete it. However, if we truly have high expectations for students, we don't let them off the hook for learning.

The use of a "Not Yet" or "Incomplete" policy for projects and assignments shifts the emphasis to learning and allows students to revise and resubmit work until it is at an acceptable level. Requiring quality work, work that meets the teacher's expectations, lets students know that the priority is learning, not simple completion of an assignment.

Recently, I spoke with Toni Eubank of the Southern Regional Education Board (SREB). As part of their comprehensive school reform model, SREB has long been a proponent of holding students to high expectations for completed work. She describes the model as Instant Credit Recovery (see Tool 140 in Chapter Five) or Instant Content Recovery.

Tool 168
The Instant Credit Recovery Model

Eight Key Elements of the Instant Credit Recovery Model

1. Teachers no longer assign grades below a C.

2. Eliminate the use of zeros.

3. Late work is late, but it must be completed if teachers are to correctly determine if students know, understand, and are able to do whatever the verb within the standard calls for.

4. Students must be given extra help opportunities (required) to learn the information, skill, or concept to complete assignments.

5. Students must retake tests that they fail and redo all assignments they earn less than a C grade on.

6. Consequences change for students not having work ready to turn in on time.

7. Grading systems change from zeros or failing grades to "I's" or some other form of non-grade.

8. A few students will still fail no matter what. The goal is to get MORE students to complete MORE assignments and assessments to the proficient level of the standard.

Tool 169
Teaching Responsibility

In one of my recent workshops, a teacher shared with me, "Our school is one of the best in our area. Parents know we have high expectations, and if students don't do the work, they receive a zero. Some of our teachers are known for the high numbers of failures, but they are also some of the most requested teachers. Zeroes and failing grades prepare our students for real life."

I asked Toni Eubank for her perspective on this issue. Her response?

Life has many do-overs, and when teachers think otherwise, they do not have a handle on the "real world" as it works today. Quality is the most important component of any job. Ask BP oil workers, their supervisors and even their now defunct CEOs. When due dates and dollars replace high-quality work, or even minimum standards, the results can be devastating. America was built on quality and innovation, and until and unless we instill these values into our students, they leave our schools with notions about "the real world" that do not actually exist in their lives. When I hear things like, "they won't get to redo work when they get on the job. They will have timelines, and if they don't do the work, they will get fired." Actually, on the job, they will have a set of expectations and responsibilities that require them to do their work at high levels and they will have to redo that work until they get it right. If they are unable to do it to begin with, they will get extra help—a lot of extra help. If the job requires knowledge and skills they do not have, they will get on-the-job training, assistance and even a mentor until they are able to do the work. Some need longer training than others, but only the inept or lazy do not make it through. If they are still unable or unwilling, they will be notified of the need for improvement, usually more than once. In most jobs, they will get verbal, then written notification of the quality of their work and of what will need to happen in order to remain on the job. If they still do not meet the work standard, then and only then will those workers be fired. Few jobs require workers to do perfect, even high quality, or even minimal work or be fired on the spot. There are steps in the firing process that must be followed.

Our current methods and the real values our schools teach students is the opposite of almost every real-world job. "If you don't do your work, you will get a zero," tells a student there is an option to do work or not. They can do the work or they can choose not to do the work. A zero is something that occurs in their future, and in this world, this generation works almost solely through instant gratification and instant consequences, students do not understand the impact of zeros, even when teachers try to tell them (Eubank, 2011, p. 2–3).

Tool 170
Sample Reassignment Policy

Robin Madden, a teacher in Rock Hill, South Carolina, shares a pilot grading policy developed by teachers at Saluda Trail Middle School and South Pointe High School. It focuses on allowing students to revise summative and formative assignments for reassessment.

Sample Reassessment Policy

♦ Students are provided at least one reassessment opportunity per major task/assessment.

♦ When reassessment is offered, all students may be reassessed, regardless of the grade on the original task/assessment. In other words, all students may re-take summative or formative assessments, as long as they re-learn the material first.

♦ Students who cheat are also allowed to re-take, but they're docked 20 percent and receive a written administrative referral.

♦ The reassessment grade should replace the original grade if it is higher than the original grade. Students are assigned the higher of the two grades.

Tool 171
Sample Rubric for Not Yet Grading

Unit VI Louisiana's Musical Landscape
Lesson 1 Music Around the State: Sound and Place

Louisiana Voices Folklife in Education Project
www.louisianavoices.org

Interpreting Music Data Rubric

Title/Topic   Louisiana's Musical Landscape   Name _____   Date _____

Task: Complete the Musical Elements Chart, the Music Genres and venues Worksheet, and the Music Prove It, and present information you learned in mural, poster, oral or written report, timeline, map, skit, or game

Performance Element	Outstanding 20 pts.	15	Great 10 pts.	5	Not yet 0 pts	Possible	Actual
Discrimination	• Listened attentively; related musical excerpts to regions of the state.		• Listened to musical excerpts, but did not relate all of them to regions of the state.		• Not attentive during listening activity; relied on others to relate music to regions of the state.	20	
Identification	• Identified all musical elements present in excerpts, identified cultural practices that affect music.		• Identified some musical elements in excerpts; cultural practices that affect music not defined for all excerpts.		• Could not identify musical elements or cultural practices.	20	

see next page

Performance Element	Outstanding 20 pts.	15	Great 10 pts.	5	Not yet 0 pts	Possible	Actual
Interpreting Information	• Categorized musical excerpts using all six musical elements; compared and contrasted recordings; recognized cultural characteristics that determine musical style.		• Categorized musical excerpts using most of the musical elements; most comparisons and contrasts were relevant; recognized some cultural characteristics that determine musical style.		• Information has not been interpreted; jumps to conclusions without carefully categorizing characteristics.	20	
Describing	• Used appropriate vocabulary to describe all genres and musical elements heard in musical excerpts.		• Described most genres and elements; some descriptions not appropriate.		• Used inappropriate descriptions for genres and elements.	20	
Disseminating Information	• Designed and created a mural, poster, oral or written report, timeline, map, skit, or game that effectively interprets the relationship of genres of music to Louisiana regions.		• Designed and created a mural, poster, oral or written report, timeline, map, skit, or game to interpret the relationship of genres of music to Louisiana regions, presentation lacking in clarity.		• Mural, poster, oral or written report, timeline, map, skit, or game not completed.	20	

Tool 172
Extra Credit Undermines Authentic Grading

When I was teaching, I struggled with the whole concept of extra credit. It never seemed to accomplish what I thought it would. The students who usually earned it didn't really need it, earning an A plus instead of an A or an A instead of a B. It also seemed to overemphasize points vs. learning.

Last year, one of my graduate students was furious because I wouldn't give her extra credit. She was on the border between an A and a B, and she wanted me to increase one low grade because she had done a good job "the rest of the time." In effect, she wanted me to give her extra credit on a very poor assignment because she wanted it.

I considered this request, as well as how a similar situation would conclude in real life. If my husband does extra work on a project for his job, he doesn't get an extra boost in his salary. It may impact his future salary or any raises, but he doesn't get an additional payment for his quality work. On the other hand, if he did a poor job on the project, he certainly doesn't get rewarded for doing something else to make up for it. In other words, extra credit isn't a part of the real world.

Tool 173
Grading for Exceptional and Struggling Learners

In *Grading Exceptional and Struggling Learners*, Lee Ann Jung and Thomas R. Guskey (2011) detail characteristics of an inclusive grading model.

1. Determine if adaptations are needed for each grade-level standard.

2. For each adaptation, determine if an accommodation or modification is needed (pull from APED to put section on this).

3. Establish the appropriate expectation for each area requiring modification.

4. Apply appropriate and equitable grading practices to the appropriate strategies.

5. Clearly communicate the meaning of the grade (ex. Footnote grade based on modified expectations).

Silva, Munk, and Bursuck (2005) also provide several suggestions when working with students with special needs:

1. Grading on individualized goals.

2. Grading based on improvement over past performance.

3. Weighting assignments differently.

4. Including indicators of effort or behavior in the grade.

5. Modifying the grading scales.

Conclusion

Assessment in a rigorous classroom can be complicated, but if you focus your efforts, you will make a difference. Using formative assessment is foundational, but assigning quality work, whether in-class or as homework, is also critical. Finally, effective grading practices will enhance the learning in your classroom.

Reflection into Action

1. What are three main tools from this chapter you could use in your classroom?

2. Which of those three will you put into place in the next three days?

3. Are there any resources you need to make this happen?

4. Which one would you like to implement next week?

5. What other tools do you want to consider for the future?

6. Is there anything else from this chapter you want to remember after you finish the book?

7
Reinvigorate the Environment

The classroom environment is basic for the other strategies throughout this book to be effective. If you think of rigor as a climbing tower, the environment is the strong foundation that allows students to climb to higher and higher levels. There are several considerations with the environment.

Emotional Environment

Adult Language

Physical Environment

Views of Success and Failure

Teacher and Student Roles

Rules and Guidelines

Emotional Environment

The emotional environment is the extent to which a student feels safe and secure in terms of feelings. You may think, "I can't control the feelings of each of my students." In reality, there are concrete ways we can help students feel better about our classrooms, which will lead to higher levels of learning.

Building a Relationship

The first step to creating a positive emotional environment is to build a relationship with your students. Understanding who they are and responding to that in supportive ways helps you connect with them. This also teaches students that you respect who they are.

Tool 174
Vision Letters

Vision letters allows students to describe their goals in a different manner. The task is to imagine it is the last day of school. Ask students to imagine that it was the best class (such as biology) or year (such as third grade) ever. What made it great? Why did they like the class so much? By reading their letters, you'll understand more about them, and probably find some ways you can adjust your instruction to best meet their needs. Also, be sure to share your vision letter with them; that way they will connect with you too!

Tool 175
Autobiographies

To encourage a positive attitude toward one another, you and your students need to understand each person. One powerful way to do this is to have students write about themselves. Sarah Ehrman explains:

> *My first assignment is* [to ask students to write an] *autobiography. It must be three typed pages, anything about themselves. Everyone wants a chance to tell their story; where they were born, about their family. They can tell me "I have a bad home situation," or "I work long hours." They write about a sport, extracurricular activities, anything they want. They are motivated when they think you want to know about them. When I started my first job, it was because the other teacher quit (it was an inner-city school teaching the "troubled" kids). They had 15 subs before I came, and they knew they were "bad kids." One of the students told other teachers* [they] *were so surprised that I cared enough to have them write 3 pages and that I cared enough to read it. I did not know that would be a big deal, but it was.*

Tool 176
Creating a Timeline

Another option is to ask students to create a timeline of experiences. After the students write their individual autobiographies, you can add photos (just take digital pictures and print them) and put them in a notebook to create a class book. It's a great way to encourage students to get to know each other better by reading the book. It's also a terrific tool for new students, parents, administrators, and substitute teachers. You can also create these electronically through a program like iBook.

Tool 177
Where I'm From Poems

An excellent strategy for getting to know students is a "Where I'm From" poem or rap. It allows students to share their lives with you, which will create a strong connection.

A great way to start these poems is to first have students organize their thoughts through simple pre-writing techniques like brainstorming, freewrites, or completing a graphic organizer. They can use the following headings to begin to brainstorm ideas: location, favorite foods, memorable moments, important people, hobbies, and favorite music. Once the students have come up with a few thoughts per heading, they can begin to put their poem together. Stress to students that perfection is not the purpose; the purpose to allow others to see you differently from what they may normally see or to learn more about you.

I Am From

I am sweet dark caramel.

I am from royalty, strong backs and bones.

I am Harriet Tubman, Martin Luther King,

Sojourner Truth, Barack Obama.

I am the creator of a legacy for which my mother and father

laid the foundation.

I am from struggles and despair.

I am love, peace, strength, courage.

I am from a place deep within my soul that makes me smile.

Abbigail Armstrong

Showing Respect

Students are more responsive to teachers who show them respect. My husband and I had a foster son several years ago. He had multiple issues with three of his four high school teachers. However, he had a great relationship with his English teacher. She had welcomed him into her classroom, and immediately commented how much she respected him for returning to school (after he had been homeless for six months). This is just another way to build relationships with your students.

Tool 178
Comments that Show Respect

One way to show respect to students is through your comments. But remember, it's not just what you say; it's how you say it!

Comments that Show Respect

I've heard you are a great artist. Will you show me some of your drawings?

I've heard some great things about your work in school.

I'm looking forward to having you in my class.

I overheard you say you like to skateboard. What do you like best about skate-boarding?

I really appreciate how you contributed to the discussion today.

Your project was excellent. I could tell you put a lot of time into it.

Caring

Caring about a student is really the summary of the two topics above. When you build a relationship with students and when you show them respect, you are actually demonstrating that you care. For students, this is truly foundational. There's an old adage, "they don't care how much you know until they know how much you care." Until students believe you care about them, nothing you do matters.

Tool 179
Showing You Care

There is a variety of ways you can show students you care about them. Just remember, if your interest is not authentic, they'll know it, and they won't respond to you in a positive manner.

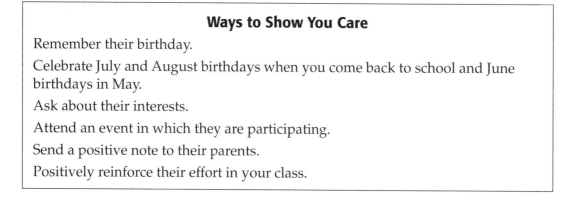

Ways to Show You Care

Remember their birthday.

Celebrate July and August birthdays when you come back to school and June birthdays in May.

Ask about their interests.

Attend an event in which they are participating.

Send a positive note to their parents.

Positively reinforce their effort in your class.

Tool 180
Personalizing Your Classroom

Barbara Bray and Kathleen McClaskey with EdTech Associates provide a perspective on personalized learning. In their view, personalized learning begins with the learner, as opposed to individualized learning which begins with the teacher. Examples of personalized learning are found in the following table. You will note that, although they focus on these characteristics starting with the learner, you could incorporate them into your classroom from your perspective, which they would consider individualized.

Characteristics of Personalized Learning

Learners actively participate in the design of their learning;

Learner chooses technology and resources to support their learning;

Learners connect with their interests, passions, and aspirations; and

Teachers develop the capacity to create independent learners who set goals, monitor progress, and reflect on learning.

Celebrating Diversity

Celebrating diversity begins when we choose to change our attitudes. We choose to recognize that having children who are different because each one is something to be valued. My grandmother loved to make quilts. One of my most cherished possessions is a quilt she made before she died. It is a patchwork kaleidoscope of colors and patterns. I love it because it is one of a kind. There has never been one like it and there will never be. It reminds me of her, an inimitable, colorful set of surprises. She would buy scraps of cloth in different stores; she didn't go in and pick everything in advance. She picked up odds and ends and then sewed them together to make this beautiful quilt.

When you celebrate diversity in your classroom, you do exactly the same thing. You take whatever you find on that first day: Some of your children are glowing, bright colors ready to learn; others are faded and dulled by their past experiences. Do you view this as good or bad? If your response is, "Great, I can mix and match these together to make a beautiful quilt," you are already on the road to celebration.

Tool 181
Culture Boxes

A creative way to learn about your students is through the use of Culture Boxes. At the beginning of the year, ask your students to put 7–10 items that represent different aspects of who they are into a shoebox. Your students will love this activity, so visit your local shoe store and get lots of shoeboxes of varying sizes. You'll have at least one student who needs the large, boot-sized box. As Charlesetta Dawson explains:

These objects reflect their family heritage, origins, ethnicity, language, religion, hobbies, and likes (foods, music, literature, movies, sports, etc.). The outsides of the boxes are decorated with pictures, symbols, and words/phrases to further explain who they are. Then the students share their culture boxes with the class. Every semester, my students always say that creating a culture box was their favorite activity because they got to be creative, share previously unknown information about themselves with their peers and teacher, and develop a better understanding of the similarities that we all have in common. The sharing might take more than one class period, but the time spent is well worth it!

Adult Language

Our adult language makes a difference to our students. Both the verbal and non-verbal language we use sends messages to students that reflect our feelings toward them.

Tool 182
Positive vs. Negative Interactions with Students

Many students have heard a lifetime of negative comments regarding their academic efforts. The words we use have a powerful impact on students. Derwin Gray, a former NFL player, says negative words are like hammering a nail into the other person. Even when we say we are sorry, which pulls the nail out, it still leaves a hole. It is important for us to respond to appropriate behaviors from students on a 4 positives to 1 negative reply or at least a 3:1 ratio in order to increase student engagement and achievement (Witzel, 2007).

Tool 183
Tracking Positive and Negative Interactions

To better understand this concept, try it for yourself. Choose a half hour period of time and count the number of positive vs. negative interactions you have with your class members. You can do this by using the chart to mark the number, place marbles in one pocket or another, or anything that works for you. Remember that smiles, frowns, and body language also count.

Positive vs. Negative Interactions

Positive Interactions	Negative Interactions

Tool 184
Turning Negatives into Positives

Next, consider the comments you have heard others say to students. What are the most negative statements you can think of? Next, consider some comments you may have used, perhaps with a less than positive tone. A more effective tool is to turn those negative comments into more encouraging ones.

Sample Negative and Positive Comments

Sample Negative Comments	Sample Positive Comments
I can't believe you did that!	Can we build on what you've done?
Are you really that stupid?	I know you can do it; let me help you.
You'll never accomplish anything.	You can accomplish anything if you work hard.
Posting a Wall of Shame	Posting a Wall of Fame

Note: The negative comments are actual samples from teachers of negative items they have seen, heard, or experienced.

Tool 185
Body Language

Our body language is also important. One of my fellow teachers during my first year of teaching told me, "Don't smile until Christmas." That isn't very good advice. Students respond to our smiles, frowns, whether or not our arms are crossed, etc. Positive body language sends a message to our students.

Positive and Negative Body Language

Positive Body Language	Negative Body Language
Smile	Frown
Arms Loose At Your Side	Crossed Arms
Standing Close to Student	Standing at a Distance
Making Eye Contact	Not Making Eye Contact

Tool 186
Praise and Encouragement

Did you know there is a difference between praise and encouragement? We use praise when a student has accomplished something. Encouragement is used when a student is attempting to learn, but struggling. Think of it this way: When a student catches a fish, we praise him or her for success. However, when a student catches a boot, we encourage her or him to keep trying.

Praise and Encouragement Statements

Praise Statements	Encouragement Statements
Congratulations on earning a B. You wrote an excellent answer for question two. You really did a great job on xxx. You are very smart and it showed on your test. I was proud of how well-behaved you were today.	That's a great start on your project. Let's take a look at this answer again. In the question it asks _____ : now how can you answer that particular part of the question? I am very proud of the effort you put forward today. I know you are disappointed that you didn't make a good grade, but it's just a start. Why don't you rework the questions you missed for partial credit.

Tool 187
Certificates

It's also effective to use certificates to recognize students' accomplishments and efforts. Customize them to meet your needs, and give them out to students to recognize their successes.

Sample Certificates

Paws for Progress

_____ showed progress

by_____

_____

Signed_____

Praise for a Peak Experience

_____ excelled at

_____

_____

Signed_____

Lighting Up with Effort

_____ put forth effort

toward_____

_____

Signed_____

Physical Environment

The physical environment of a rigorous classroom is positive, welcoming, safe, and focused on progress. The physical aspects of your room are a critical part of an environment that supports rigor.

Tool 188
Success Quotes

In order to reinforce the positive, post positive quotes about success around the room.

Sample Positive Quotes

"Whether you think you can or you can't, you're right." (Henry Ford)

"Every great dream begins with a dreamer. Always remember, you have within you the strength, the patience, and the passion to reach for the stars to change the world." (Harriet Tubman)

"Defeat is not the worst of failures. Not to have tried is the true failure." (George Edward Woodberry)

"I've failed over and over again in my life and that is why I succeed." (Michael Jordan)

"It is our choices that show what we truly are, far more than our abilities." (J. K. Rowling)

"In order to succeed, your desire for success should be greater than your fear of failure." (Bill Cosby)

"We are what we repeatedly do. Excellence, therefore, is not an act but a habit." (Aristotle)

"It always seems impossible until it's done." (Nelson Mandela)

"No one can make you feel inferior without your consent." (Eleanor Roosevelt)

Tool 189
Positive Role Models

Students also need to see positive role models. Many of the students you teach either don't have a role model for the future, or the one(s) they have do not value education or long-term goals. Read about, talk about, and visibly reinforce role models that can be a positive influence on your students.

```
Sample Role Models
Oprah Winfrey
Tyler Perry
Demi Levato (singer who fights against bullying)
Jay-Z
Martin Luther King
Dr. Oz
Dwayne Wade
Jennifer Lopez
Eva Longoria
```

Please note: *These are current at the time of publication but people (and whether or not they are appropriate role models) can change. Use an up-to-date list in your classroom.*

Tool 190
Student Role Models

As we have already discussed, it's important to post pictures and stories of role models. Tool 189 provided a list of famous role models to use in your classroom. However, another alternative is to use your students as role models. Create posters following the template below and post around your room.

Template for Student Role Model Poster

Name	
Picture of Student	Interests
Goals	Favorite Subject (and why)

Tool 191
Welcome Doors

A simple way to welcome students to your room is to decorate your door. You can use a theme, or just words, but the message is clear: I want you here to learn!

Ideas for Door Themes

Oh The Places You Will Go with students' faces on tiny balloons with a welcome message.

Rainbow Fish and student's faces can make up the scales. The message should encourage diversity (the rainbow fish has many colors). For example: We Like Different!!

Olympic Medalist with students' names on gold medals including a message about Winners Enter Here or Success in Progress.

Construction Zone: Science Skill Building in Progress (can choose your topic)

Use a popular song like "Call Me Maybe" by Carly Rae Jepsen except change the lyrics to "Read Me Maybe."

Tool 192
Welcome Notes

At the start of the year, you can tape a welcome note to students' desks or tables. When you have multiple classes, use a generic statement; when possible, use a student's name.

Sample Phrases for Welcome Messages

Welcome to my class!

We're going to have a great year!

Thanks for being a positive part of our classroom!

Tool 193
Posting Key Information

Another key aspect of the physical environment is using your walls, whiteboards, etc. for information. If there is critical reference information students will need, post this in a spot that is clearly visible and available to students.

Examples of Critical Information

Steps in the Scientific Process

Characteristics of Good Employees

Elements of a Book

Parts of Speech

Types of Government

Tool 194
Posting Strategic Information

In addition to reference information, there is strategic information that is important to students. These are reminders about learning strategies (see Chapter 5) that should also be posted. In my classroom, I posted a set of guidelines to follow when students did not know a particular vocabulary word.

How to Figure Out a Word You Don't Know

Try to figure it out on your own.

Read the sentence to understand the meaning.

Look for prefixes or suffixes that you know to help you understand the word.

Check to see whether the word is in the glossary or margin of the book.

Look it up in the dictionary.

Use a thesaurus.

Ask three other students for help.

If nothing else works, ask the teacher.

Another example is critical information related to safety in a science classroom. Items such as this should be prominently posted throughout the year.

Safety Procedures

1. STUDENTS MAY NOT WORK IN THE LABORATORY WITHOUT A CERTIFIED SCIENCE INSTRUCTOR PRESENT.

2. Only students registered for the class are allowed in the laboratory.

3. No backpacks or purses are allowed in the laboratory area.

4. Do not handle equipment and supplies set up in the laboratory until given instruction to do so from the instructor.

5. Clothing and attire should provide protection from hazardous substances.

6. Eye protection must be worn when required by the lab instructor. Students must purchase safety goggles approved for use by AASD.

7. Personal protective equipment such as gloves and a laboratory apron should be used at the direction of the laboratory instructor.

8. No eating or drinking is permitted in any science classroom unless a consumable is part of a laboratory procedure and the instructor gives permission to eat the consumable.

9. Never place anything in the mouth while in the laboratory except as directed by the instructor.

10. Smell chemicals only by wafting a small amount of vapor toward the nose with the hand.

11. No unauthorized experimentation is allowed. Do not change written laboratory procedures without the permission of the instructor.

12. Follow laboratory procedures *carefully and accurately*. Do not proceed with any experiment if you do not understand the procedure.

13. All chemical names and identities should be carefully double-checked prior to use.

14. Laboratory fume hoods should be used for all operations which have the potential to release fumes, gasses, or volatile solvent vapors in excess of recommended exposure levels. Notify the instructor if you think the fume hood is not functioning properly.

15. Clean up spills promptly. If you have questions on spill clean up, ask the instructor. Do not attempt to clean up spilled mercury. Notify the instructor immediately.

16. Clean up broken glass using a broom and dustpan and dispose of in the proper container, NOT in the wastebasket.

17. Proper disposal of laboratory waste is essential. Do not dispose of any chemical in the sink without approval from the instructor. Use appropriate waste containers when provided.

18. Students should clean the work area and wash hands thoroughly before leaving the room.

19. Report all injuries, no matter how minor, to the instructor. The instructor will give guidance on the treatment needed and direct the student to the health room, if needed.

Safety Equipment:

20. Students should know the location of and how to operate all available safety equipment. This includes: eye wash stations, safety showers, fire extinguishers, fire blankets, first aid supplies, and master shutoffs for gas, electricity and water.

21. Students should know the location of emergency telephone numbers and how to use them.

Source: www.aasd.k12.wi.us/staff/Leonardann/safety.htm

Tool 195
Following Directions

An Illinois teacher in one of my workshops shared that he posts a simple reminder on his wall.

WIDFD

It stands for: When in Doubt, Follow Directions. Following directions is another strategy that is not a strong point for many students. In this case, the teacher used a simple acronym to remind his students to follow directions.

Tool 196
Working in Groups

Another strategy that students may not understand is that of working in small groups. Too often, students just sit with other students and complete work individually, which is not cooperative or collaborative learning. It is important to model for students effective group work, perhaps through a video, as well as providing clear guidelines for students. In the following tables, you'll see two rubrics for cooperative learning that can assist you in teaching your students the strategy of effective group work.

Cooperative Learning Rubrics

Cooperative learning Rubric			
	You're a Team Player!	**You're Working on It...**	**You're Flying Solo**
G Group dedication	The student is totally dedicated to his or her group, offering all of his or her attention by actively listening to peers and responding with ideas.	The student is partially dedicated to his or her group though sometimes becomes distracted by students or issues outside the group.	The student spends most of his or her time focusing on things outside the group; he or she is not available for discussion or group work.
R Responsibility	The student shares responsibility equally with other group members and accepts his or her role in the group.	The student takes on responsibility but does not completely fulfill his or her obligations.	The student either tries to take over the group and does not share responsibilities or takes no part at all in the group work assigned.
O Open communication	The student gives polite and constructive criticism to group members when necessary, welcomes feedback from peers, resolves conflict peacefully, and asks questions when a group goal is unclear.	The student gives criticism, though often in a blunt manner, reluctantly accepts criticism from peers, and may not resolve conflict peacefully all of the time.	The student is quick to point out the faults of other group members yet is unwilling to take any criticism in return; often, the students argues with peers rather than calmly coming to a consensus.
U Utilization of work time	The student is always on task, working with group members to achieve goals, objectives, and deadlines.	The student is on task most of the time but occasionally takes time off from working with the group.	The student does not pay attention to the task at hand and frustrates other group members because of his or her inability to complete work in a timely fashion.
P Participation	The student is observed sharing ideas, reporting research findings to the group, taking notes from other members, and offering assistance to his or her peers as needed.	The student sometimes shares ideas or reports findings openly but rarely takes notes from other group members.	This student does not openly share ideas or findings with the group, nor does he or she take notes on peers'

Student Cooperative Learning Rubric (Elementary)			
	You're a Team Player **3**	You're Working on It... **2**	You're the Lone Ranger **1**	Total for Each Category
G Group Dedication	I listened respectfully to my teammates' ideas and offered suggestions that helped my group.	I did listen to ideas, but I didn't give suggestions.	I was distracted and more interested in the other groups than my group.	**Group Dedication** I circled number 3 2 1
R Responsibility	I eagerly accepted responsibility with my group and tried to do my part to help everyone in my group.	I accepted responsibility within my group without arguing.	I quarreled and did not accept roles given by my group.	**Responsibility** I circled number 3 2 1
O Open Communication	I listened to others' ideas and tried to solve conflicts peacefully.	I listened to others' ideas, but did not try to solve conflicts.	I was controlling and argumentative to my group.	**Open Communication** I circled number 3 2 1
U Use of Work Time	I was involved and engaged; I encouraged my group the entire time we were working.	I tried my best the entire time we were working.	I was not involved and did not offer any suggestions for the good of the group.	**Use of Work Time** I circled number 3 2 1
P Participation	I was a team member. I offered ideas, suggestions, and help for my group.	I participated in the project, but did not offer to help anyone.	I did not participate because I was not interested.	**Participation** I circled number 3 2 1
				Total_____

For a sample rubric for older students, visit: www.barbarablackburnonline.com/PDF/Class roomInstruction/CoplearningRubric.pdf

Views of Success and Failure

Students view success and failure in various ways. For example, I taught a student who thought any success she had was due to luck. When I tried to convince her otherwise, she said, "I guess you gave me my grade, right?" She never saw the connection between her work and her success. In a similar manner, I had a student who never thought failure was his fault. There was always another reason he failed.

Tool 197
Students' Perspectives of Failure vs. Success

Students who are strategic in their understanding differ from those who struggle with learning. In the following table, you'll see the difference in the material adapted from Steve Siebold (www.stevesiebold.com).

How Strategic and Non-Strategic Students View Success

Non-Strategic Learners	Strategic Learners
Doesn't think about thinking (no metacognition).	Thinks about thinking—a lot, even without realizing it (metacognition).
Perspective of Self and Others	
Places high value on the opinions of others (needs constant reassurance).	Is confident of own decisions.
External frame of reference.	Internal locus of control.
Asks for help first without trying to work out problem on own.	Asks for help only after uses toolkit of own strategies.
Connections	
Doesn't connect learning to other things unless made explicit by the teacher—doesn't realize that all connects to long-term.	Thinks about the "what if . . ." always making connections in head to self; other learning experiences; and future/real life.
Cannot visualize an end product or a correct result of task or learning—doesn't know what it "feels like to be right."	Can visualize the end product or result of task or learning—is confident of correctness and/or being right.
Views About Failure	
Views failure as the end—not as a learning process.	Learns from failures/views failure as a learning process.
Used feedback and criticism as a stop sign.	Used feedback and criticism to improve.
Problems and Solutions	
No plans for what to do if what they are told to do doesn't work.	Plans for the unexpected—and deals with those things/alternative plans.
Overwhelmed by problems.	Deals with one problem at a time.

Tool 198
Moving from Failure to Success

Once you are aware of your students' perspectives, you can help students move from a failure perspective to one of success.

Strategies to Help Students Move to a Perspective of Success

View of Failure	Strategy
Perspective of Self and Others	Don't just give student the answer; ask why questions to encourage him/her to figure it out of his/her own. Allow limited questioning of other students. For example, allow the student to ask two other students for help, but no more. Discourage dependency and learned helplessness. Reinforce independence as much as possible.
Connections	Use graphic organizers to help students make connections. Model connections through think-alouds so students can learn what to do. Continually ask questions that require students to make connections to other learning. Show models of the end product expected so students can know what to do.
Views about Failure	Focus on progress as well as achievement. Encourage effort. Share examples of other failures that have led to success (either with public figures or yourself).
Problems and Solutions	Chunk problems into smaller parts. Encourage looking at problems in different ways. Ask "what if." Reinforce effort.

Goals and Success

Students need to set and achieve goals to build a sense of confidence, which leads to a willingness to try something else, which in turn begins a cycle that leads to higher levels of success. Success leads to success, and the achievements of small goals are building blocks to larger goals. Successful goal setting is a crucial part of a rigorous classroom.

Tool 199
SMART Goals

The model of setting SMART goals is effective because they are simple and understandable for students.

Let's look at how this works with students' goals. Peter is a high achiever who wants to be perfect. In fact, if you ask him for his goal, he'll say it is to be a perfect

SMART Goals

S Specific

M Measurable

A Attainable

R Realistic

T Timely

student. But that isn't specific or measurable because perfection is subjective and difficult to measure. It is probably not attainable or realistic because perfection is such an elusive goal; and it isn't timely because there is no end date. This sets Peter up for failure, because there is no way to achieve the goal and move on to the next one.

I also like the SMART goals approach because it forces you and/or your students to break down the specific steps needed to achieve the goal. I watched a parent respond to the following comment from a teacher: "Your daughter needs to study harder to do well in my class." He replied, "My daughter *is* studying hard. What do you mean study harder?" This parent was looking for actions he could control, and the vague nature of the statement frustrated him. It is more helpful to describe the specific next actions to take. Think of items on a list that can be checked off when they are completed.

We know what those are. By *study harder*, we really mean things like read the text selection, take notes in class and study them at home; do your homework every night and if you have a question, first try to find the answer, then ask the teacher; and don't wait until the last minute to work on a project, work on it a little every night. The problem is that we don't always say these things to parents or students, or we say them once and don't provide further reminders.

Tool 200
Goal-Setting Activities

A good place to start is to talk about goals with students. You can share one of your goals, and discuss their goals. You may have to start broader with dreams, and then focus on the specific goals. I visited a classroom that had a large bulletin board titled "Our Goals." Each student wrote his or her goal and posted it for everyone to see. Many wrote the standard "make good grades," but some wrote more personal ones. Other options are to have students write about their goals in journals. The point is to have them identify their own goals and for you to know about them so you can tie learning to their goals.

I used two different goal-setting activities when I was teaching. First, each of my students created a "Me Poster" at the start of the year. I adapted this idea from one my dad used with teachers during workshops. I provided some starting points using basic pictures or shapes, and they could customize the posters. This gave me a tremendous amount of information about who they were and their interests and goals—probably more than I would have known if I had merely talked with them, or even asked them to write about themselves because many were reluctant writers.

Components of a Me Poster

Star—In what way do you star as a student?

Trading Stamp—What part of your personality would you like to trade in?

Flower Pot—How can you make our classroom a better place to be?

First Prize Ribbon—For what one thing would you like to be remembered?

Crown—What is your crowning achievement?

Winner Sign—Why are you a winner?

Turkey—What are the turkeys that get you down?

Question Mark—What one thing do you want others to know about you?

My students and I also enjoyed creating time capsules for each person using paper towel cardboard rolls. At the start of the school year, I asked them to focus on where they were in terms of academics, accomplishments, or interests. Students selected objects that represented different things about themselves, and they put those objects in the tube along with an essay they wrote. They told about themselves using the contents, then filled the tube and decorated it. I hung the tubes in the classroom, and at the end of the year, my students opened them and wrote a new essay about how they had changed over the year. Many of them were surprised at how much they had learned and grown.

Tool 201
Victory List

One way to track success toward goals is to have your students keep a Victory List. This can be in the back of their journals or student agendas; it just needs to be somewhere they can readily access it. A Victory List is simply a personal list of successes. It includes items such as:

- I made a B on my paper.

- I drew a good picture.

- I didn't fight with Joaquim.

- I remembered that if I draw something, it helps me learn a new word.

- I took my paper home and my sister was proud of me.

The purpose of a victory list is to help us remember what we have accomplished, particularly when things aren't going so well. Sometimes when we're struggling, we forget all that we've accomplished. Keeping a concrete list of successes is a constant visual reminder of progress.

Tool 202
Encouraging Effort

As students are required to work at more rigorous levels, the role of effort becomes more important. It is likely that with more rigorous work, students will not automatically be successful. Therefore, they will need to put forth more effort. For many students, rather than continuing to persist, they will give up. Instead, we need to encourage effort.

In *Classroom Instruction That Works* (2001), Marzano, Pickering, and Pollock make two important comments about students' views about effort.

Research-Based Generalizations About Effort

1. Not all students realize the importance of believing in effort.
2. Students can learn to change their beliefs to an emphasis on effort (Marzano et al., 2001, p. 50).

In short, if we teach students the importance of effort, and reinforce it throughout our lessons, students can learn to put forth more effort.

Tool 203
Praising Effort vs. Ability

When she was at Columbia University, Carol Dweck investigated the role of praise and student achievement (http://nymag.com/news/features/27840/). She discovered an interesting point. When we only praise students for being smart, they put forth less effort, and in the long run, have lower achievement. On the other hand, when students are praised for their effort, they put forth more effort and increase their achievement over time. In other words, students who consider their ability to be the indicator of their success assume they don't need to try. On the other hand, students who are praised for their determination to work through their struggles continue to work hard to achieve.

This does not mean that you can never praise a student for their ability. However, next time you're tempted to say, "Madeline, you're so smart!", remember to add, "And you worked so hard on this project!"

Teacher and Student Roles

In a rigorous environment, the teacher's role changes to one that is less direct and more facilitative.

Tool 204
Teacher as Facilitator

Do you manage your classroom or do you facilitate instruction? In a rigorous classroom, ownership is shifted to students; therefore, the teacher's role changes. Rather than directing everything that is happening, the teacher assists as students begin to lead their own instruction.

Teacher as Manager	Teacher as Facilitator
Teacher directs instruction. Teacher is in charge. Teacher asks questions. Teacher lectures. Teacher controls activities.	Teacher facilitates instruction. Teacher shifts leadership to students. Teacher leads discussion. Ownership is shifted to students.

Student Ownership of Learning

In a community of learners, students share ownership or participation in learning. In this model most students are more motivated, and thrive in their learning.

Tool 205
Elements of Student Ownership

There are three elements of student ownership: choice, voice, and leadership.

Ways to Allow Student Ownership

Element of Ownership	Examples
Choice	Choice in how to demonstrating learning Choice in projects Choice in reading materials Choice in assignments
Voice	Have input in the way the lesson will be taught Make recommendations as to appropriate resources for lesson Help determine the order of topics within a lesson (if appropriate)
Leadership	Helping teach a lesson Leading small groups Helping teacher Teach other students

Rules and Guidelines

Finally, rules and guidelines are an important part of a rigorous environment. It's important to remember that there is a purpose for rules and guidelines: to help students feel safe and secure. Develop guidelines, ideally with student input for ownership, and reinforce them fairly.

Tool 206
Helping Students Feel Safe and Secure

Your rules, procedures, and guidelines do not have to be lengthy, but they do need to be clear and understandable to students. Without clear expectations, students cannot be held accountable. However, be prepared to reinforce the rules; otherwise, students learn they do not have to follow them.

Sample Rules

Be respectful of yourself and others.

Be prepared.

Follow directions.

Keep hands, feet, and objects to yourself.

Do your best.

Tool 207
Student-Created Rules

In many democratic classrooms, teachers work with students to develop rules. In this case, the teacher facilitates a discussion of what it means to respect each other and the teacher. Then, he or she asks students what they believe respect looks like in the classroom. From that discussion, the teacher writes the agreed upon rules. Involving students in the creation process builds student ownership in the learning environment.

Conclusion

Reinvigorating your classroom environment to reinforce rigor does not mean starting from scratch. You likely have many of these elements already in place; it's just a matter of incorporating new ideas, and consistently implementing others.

Reflection into Action

1. What are three main tools from this chapter you could use in your classroom?

2. Which of those three will you put into place in the next three days?

3. Are there any resources you need to make this happen?

4. Which one would you like to implement next week?

5. What other tools do you want to consider for the future?

6. Is there anything else from this chapter you want to remember after you finish the book?

8
Extend Your Reach

Finally, let's turn our attention to extending your reach outside your immediate classroom. Whether you want support for your efforts, or you want to share your successes with others, it's important to involve various stakeholder groups. We'll look at working with parents and families, administrators including instructional specialists, your school board, and other teachers.

> **Parents and Families**
>
> Administrators
> Instructional Specialists
> School Board
> Other Teachers

Working with Parents and Families

Partnering with the parents and families of your students provides advantages to you, your students, and to their families. Families will have a better idea of what's happening in school, which also allows them to help support their son or daughter at home. Students benefit when they receive encouragement at home. And teachers benefit when learning is reinforced and supported by parents and families. Let's discuss how to PAIR with parents and families to improve student learning. Please note that I'll be using the word "parents," but consider it all-inclusive with families.

Tool 208
PAIR with Parents

PAIR

Partnerships are a Two-Way Street

Accentuate the Positive

Inform and Transform

Relationships are Shared

Partnerships are a Two-Way Street

A true partnership is more than communication from school to home. Although it's our responsibility to take the initiative to form partnerships, everyone has a role. I've found that most parents are willing to help, but they need specific ways to help.

Kendra Alston, a teacher in Charlotte-Mecklenburg Schools in North Carolina, sends home an interactive newsletter every two weeks. Besides the information, there is a question for the parents to answer and send back. She has a high return rate because students receive points for returning the newsletter. She also uses interactive homework. "For example, I'll take a picture of something my students did in school. Then, I write 'Ask me what I learned today' at the top of the page. The parents have to write what their son or daughter said. This lets me know if the students even remember what happened. I'm also always about getting feedback on my own performance and when the parent writes a reflection on what their child is learning, it gives you insight on how well you taught."

It's also helpful to provide parents a list of ways they can help at home. This should include clear guidelines of what constitutes appropriate help (doing their science project for them isn't) and any other simple tips (see Tool 209, General Tips for Parents). Many elementary schools send home a monthly calendar to post on the refrigerator. Each day has a simple activity families can do together.

Tool 209
General Tips for Parents

General Tips for Parents

Encourage your son or daughter to give 100 percent at all times.

Reinforce concepts and habits the teacher is trying to build. If Jonathan is learning how to multiply percents at school, have him help you calculate the tip at a restaurant.

Encourage your son or daughter to set a designated time when homework will be completed every day.

Provide a quiet, well-lit environment at home with all of the materials necessary for completing school tasks (extra paper, scissors, pens, pencils, pencil sharpener, a dictionary, markers, highlighters, a ruler, calculator, index cards, etc.).

Prevent brain freeze—allow your son or daughter to take a short break every thirty minutes or between homework tasks.

Be careful not to give answers to homework questions; instead, offer advice about where to look for an answer.

Model what productive work looks like. When your son or daughter does homework, you do yours too (balance a checkbook, pay the bills, etc.).

Tool 210
Rigor Tip Sheet for Parents

It's also important to let parents know how they can incorporate rigor at home.

Rigor Tip Sheet for Parents

1. Rigor is simple to implement in school and at home.
2. Rigor is NOT moving your son or daughter to another grade level.
3. Rigor is being challenged on grade level but support is provided like reading guides to help students navigate through difficult or unfamiliar text.
4. Rigor is helping your son or daughter think for him or herself. You can help your son or daughter do this being teaching him to think beyond the text, by asking questions starting with "What if . . . ?"
5. Rigor is helping your son or daughter make connections among the disciplines. Ask, "How does this topic relate to what you are studying in your other classes?"
6. Rigor is allowing your son or daughter to explore and discover. It is okay if he takes a while to get the answer and you can see it clearly. Home is the appropriate place for your son or daughter to take his time and process while solving problems.
7. Rigor is providing guidance not answers. When your son or daughter asks for help, provide guidance, not answers. Too much help teaches that someone will do the work for him or her.
8. Rigor is providing a supportive environment at home for your son or daughter to work. He or she needs to know it is okay if his or her answers are not

perfect and that he/she can ask for help as long as he/she has exhausted other measures such as checking class notes, looking to her text or other reading material or doing some light research online.

9. Rigor is using and teaching your son or daughter to use positive language when confronted with a challenge. "I can't" are not words anyone may use in your own. Instead say, "I am having trouble getting this done. I am going to try to do it by myself, but I may need some help."

10. Rigor is having high expectations for your son or daughter and cheering them on when they are frustrated or challenged.

Accentuate the Positive

I called every parent during the first month of school to introduce myself and tell them something positive about their son or daughter. I thought of parent relationships like a bank; I needed to make a deposit before I made a withdrawal. I didn't want my first phone call to be the one about a poor grade or a discipline problem. One time it took 17 calls to reach a parent before I was finally successful. It took about five minutes to convince her I wasn't calling because Marcus was in trouble. She finally said she had never received a call from a teacher telling her something positive about her son. She thanked me and immediately offered her help anytime I needed it. Five weeks later when Marcus was in trouble in class, she supported me 100 percent. Focusing on the positive has benefits for you, your students, and their parents.

Tool 211
Ways to Share Positive News Through Social Media

There are many social media tools you can use to communicate with parents and to share positive news. As a caution, be sure you are protecting the privacy of your classroom and your students. For example, on Pinterest, don't name your boards with your location or your full name. Also, there are private blogs that require invitations or membership, so you can control who sees the information.

Social Media Tools for Sharing Positive News

Pinterest to share samples of student work (code or remove names for privacy; do not post grades).

Blog to share descriptions of the positive things going on in your classroom.

Tumblr to share videos of class activities and presentations (remember to get permission for recording).

Inform and Transform

When I talk to parents, many of them feel as though there is a hidden code in schools; a code they don't understand. Margo and her son moved to a new area when Jared started middle school. She missed the first parent-teacher meeting because she was working. She called the school and left several messages asking to meet with his teachers, but didn't receive a return call. Margo was frustrated when she told me her story. Another teacher at the school was in one of my classes, so I talked with her. I discovered that the school had a policy that all appointments with teachers were scheduled with the attendance secretary, so the entire teaching team could meet with parents without scheduling conflicts. My graduate student said the principal always explained the policy at the first meeting. So, of course, Margo didn't know because she wasn't at the meeting, and she thought the teachers were just ignoring her. One phone call later, she connected with the teachers, and she and Jared finished the year successfully.

Tool 212
Parent Brochure

Building partnerships with parents is founded on informing parents about what is going on in your classrooms, which transforms the relationship. You want parents to feel that they are truly a part of your classroom. And that can't happen if they don't know or understand what you are doing. Kendra believes that communication is an important part of her job. During the first two weeks of school, she guides her students as they create a brochure for parents about their classroom.

"The students do all preliminaries, I just put it together. I tell them my philosophy, then each block gets together and comes up with quote that describes their class. It also includes a poem I write to parents every year that finishes by asking for support from them. I always finish with the message that I can't do anything without you." Kendra also sends a brochure that informs parents of basic information they need during the year, including her contact information, grading and homework information, and any other relevant classroom policies (see the sample brochure text under Tool 213).

Tool 213
Rigor Column

I think it's important to send home a brochure or other written information that provides parents with key information. In your brochure, include a column on rigor.

> *This quarter in* Education News *rigor is our hot topic! Rigor is a positive concept that should be used in classrooms no matter the ability of the students. When teachers practice the use of rigor, our students are challenged but with adequate support. A good everyday definition is that rigor is high expectations plus support plus student demonstration of learning. I'll use rigor in my classroom by increasing the level of reading students will do, but also by providing aids such as reading guides so students can navigate through a piece of text more easily or a graphic organizer to help them solve a problem in mathematics. You can provide rigor by requiring your son or daughter to discuss material read in language arts, math, science, or social studies by giving a summary. You can also require your son or daughter to explain how they got a solution for a mathematics problem or describe the process they chose to complete a science experiment. Rigor is really all about learning; helping your son or daughter learn at higher levels. I look forward to our year!*

Relationships are Shared

Many partnerships are destroyed before they start, because the teacher believes it is someone else's responsibility to prompt a connection. This was exactly the attitude of my former colleague. If you believe it's the parents' responsibility to communicate and/or follow-up with you, that attitude comes through when you talk with them. Communicating with parents is not an extra job; it is part of your job. There is no way you can truly help your students be successful without the support of their parents. And it's up to you to take the first step. Suzanne Okey, a former teacher of students with special needs, points out that sometimes PTA meetings and phone calls are not enough.

> *In terms of families, I'm big on home visits. I feel like it's always fair to get off your turf and go into the environment where they are most comfortable. It says this is a two way street; I'm not expecting you to make all the accommodations; I'll meet you where you are. If teachers truly want to form partnerships, they cannot expect it all to be "come to me;" you have to be willing to go to them. Sometimes I sent a letter. It is important to give them options, such as meeting them in neutral places (the public library or McDonald's) in order to preserve their privacy and dignity. Not everyone has transportation or telephones, and they don't want to advertise that to world.*

It's our responsibility to connect with parents; and the benefits outweigh any costs in terms of time.

Tool 214
Parent–Teacher Meetings

You may want to present information about rigor at a parent/family–teacher meeting. It's important to tailor your presentation to your audience. For example, if you have a large number of college-educated and/or college-oriented parents, then you should incorporate more information about preparing for college.

Sample Agenda for Parent–Teacher Meeting

Opening Activity: Using stickers, ask parents to choose yes/no for each of the following thoughts:

- I want my son/daughter to be challenged to learn new things.

- I want teachers to help my son/daughter learn more.

- I want my son/daughter to have chances to show what they know.

- I want my son/daughter to be ready for <choose appropriate options> life, college, a job, middle school, high school, the next grade level.

As you present information, incorporate the responses to the questions. For example, as you talk about rigor including challenging activities, you can say, "100 percent of you said you want your son/daughter to be challenged to learn new things."

Presentation: Use the categories and bulleted points to present information you've learned about in this book. An accompanying PowerPoint is available for your use at http://www.routledge.com/books/details/9780415732871/

Why is rigor important?

- Prepare students for the future (jobs, college, etc.).

- Help them learn new and challenging material. This is the purpose of school, not just to repeat what they have already learned.

What is rigor?

- Challenging students to high expectations for learning, helping them learn, and letting them show how much they understand.

- Alternative is to use my formal definition: creating an environment in which each student is expected to learn at high levels; each student is supported so he or she can learn at high levels; and each student demonstrates learning at high levels.

What are some examples that we'll see in the classrooms?

- Instruction will include questions that require thinking and they may have more than one answer (give samples appropriate to grade levels and subjects).

- We'll be reading more than one book, sometimes at the same time, so students can compare them to each other.

- When they answer a question, students will be asked to show where they found the answer in the story/article/text.

- Your sons and daughters will be writing a lot!

- They'll be using problem-solving in math, not just memorizing facts.

♦ On their homework, they will be asked to explain their answers.

♦ If something is too easy, we'll move your son/daughter to more challenging work. The goal is higher learning.

What about grades?

♦ We focus on learning more than grades.

♦ There will still be a grading scale (A, B, C, etc.) or standards-based grading (choose what you will use).

♦ If work is challenging, your son/daughter probably won't make 100 on everything.

♦ However, they can still make an A.

♦ If using redo policy (see Tool 169 in Chapter Six): At times, students will be given the opportunity to redo work to show understanding and improve grades. In real life, you probably get more than one chance to be successful. So will our students (see more at Tool 169 in Chapter Six).

What can I do as a parent/family member?

♦ Praise for effort and progress.

♦ Don't panic over a couple of lower grades; look at overall work.

♦ Encourage your son/daughter to keep up with and do their best work.

♦ If you son or daughter asks you to look at their homework and tell them if it's "right," ask them to explain their answer before you tell them.

♦ If a teacher asks students to redo work, that is positive. It gives them more time to take advantage of extra help and another chance to show they understand the content and improve their grades.

♦ Talk to the teacher(s). It always helps to understand what is happening.

♦ Remember, we want to challenge each student to do his or her best.

♦ Hand out tip sheet (Tool 210).

Questions and Answers

♦ Take questions from the group and provide follow-up.

Working with Administrators

Working with your administrators is a critical part of your success as a teacher. In addition to needing their support when there is a conflict with parents, they can be of tremendous help when you are implementing new strategies.

Tool 215
Helping Your Administrator Understand Rigor

During a recent workshop I led in Florida, a teacher stayed afterward to talk with me. She said that earlier in the week she had tried one of the activities I shared, but that her administrator noted during the observation that it was not rigorous. "What do I do?", she asked.

I suggested that, when she returned to school, she have a conversation with her principal—one that was positive and constructive, not critical. Here's a sample of what we decided she would say:

I would like to talk with you about the questioning game my students played during my observation. When we talked, you mentioned that it was not rigorous. I'd like to explain why I think it was rigorous. I just returned from a workshop on rigor, and the same activity was used as an example of rigorous work. Do you mind if I share what the presenter said about how the activity was rigorous?

First, even though some of the question prompts used were at lower levels of Bloom's Taxonomy, they led to extended discussions. Also, the majority of the prompts students used to create questions were higher order ones.

Next, the students created questions rather than simply answering my questions. Since it is more difficult to create questions than to answer them, students were required to truly understand the content to participate in the activity.

Finally, each student was required to demonstrate understanding of content. Sometimes, I've asked questions and called on students to answer. This means that other students may or may not understand—I don't know since they didn't answer. By working in small groups, everyone participates. Even with one student asking the question, the other three discuss the answer. And each student must create multiple questions.

The use of higher order questions, analysis and reflection required to create questions, and the student-centered nature of the activity combined to make the questioning game rigorous.

The teacher emailed me two days later. Her principal was open to the conversation and responded positively to her comments, which resulted in a change on her evaluation. I've repeatedly found that teachers and administrators don't always know what makes something rigorous. In this case, the principal equated rigor with higher order questions, and when she saw students asking a mix of questions, she thought it wasn't rigorous. The teacher knew it was a rigorous activity, but couldn't explain why. With this conversation, everyone was on the same page.

Tool 216
Six Steps for Gaining Support for Your Plan

As you consider working with your administrators, it's critical to let them know what you are doing related to rigor. Of course, if your plan is part of a school-wide or district-wide initiative, then you may not need to work through all these steps. But I do encourage you to keep the lines of communication open. I've found that most administrators want to support high expectations, student scaffolding, and student demonstration of learning—in other words, rigor; but they don't like surprises! As one principal shared with me, "My concern is when I hear about something new from a parent before I hear about it from the teacher."

For you to be successful in increasing rigor, you want administrative support. This is particularly true if or when you get pushback from parents and/or students. I recommend you use a six step process as you collaborate with your principal and other administrators.

Six Steps
1. Goal
2. Purpose
3. Process
4. Support
5. Successes
6. Feedback

Step 1: Goal

What is your goal? I recommend you be more specific than to "increase rigor." Here are three sample goals:

1. Increase my expectations by incorporating Webb's Depth of Knowledge.

2. Develop and implement a toolkit of additional scaffolding strategies.

3. Develop common assessments with my team/grade level/department.

Step 2: Purpose

Your purpose is linked to your goal, but it is a little broader. For example, my purpose in incorporating Webb's Depth of Knowledge is to move my students into more complex work, such as analyzing multiple texts, synthesizing information, and creating my own argumentative essay based on the work. Or, by using additional scaffolding strategies, I hope to increase student understanding throughout the lesson. Finally, by developing common assessments, I'll help ensure that my students will demonstrate learning at a higher level.

Step 3: Process

Now you move to the details; what steps will you follow to put your plan into place?

Area	Steps
Incorporating Webb's Depth of Knowledge	• Review materials on DOK. • Google sample lesson plans using DOK. • Review current lessons. • Revise to incorporate DOK. • Implement lessons. • Adjust on ongoing basis.
Develop/Implement Additional Scaffolding	• Ask other teachers for most effective scaffolding strategies. • Meet with instructional coach to discuss scaffolding strategies. • Review current lessons. • Revise to incorporate additional scaffolding. • Implement lessons. • Ask instructional coach to observe/ provide informal feedback. • Adjust on ongoing basis.
Develop/Implement Common Assessments	• Contact other teachers to agree to work on this project (completed). • Schedule meetings or time within current meetings to work on project. • Choose one standard and ask everyone to develop a rigorous assessment for that standard. • During meeting, compare assessments and combine to create common one. • All teachers in the group implement assessment. • Meet to provide feedback and make adjustments. • Repeat (goal is to create at least two common assessments this year).

Step 4: Support

Then, ask for any support you need. In the case of incorporating Webb's Depth of Knowledge, you may need training, or you may just need some encouragement. With scaffolding, you may want your principal to purchase several books as resources, or you might ask for time with the instructional specialist. In the case of the common assessments, you might need help finding and scheduling common time for your Professional Learning Community to develop the assessments.

Step 5: Share Successes

If you have already implemented aspects of your plan, share the successes you have experienced, as well as how they have shaped your desire to move forward. If you are just starting or are continuing, share your successes on a regular basis. Not only will this encourage you, it will demonstrate the benefits of your plan to your administrator(s).

Step 6: Feedback

Finally, as you begin, and again throughout the process, ask for feedback. Be open to suggestions that will help you improve. Another view is always beneficial. Feedback is a valuable tool for your own professional growth and the success of your plan.

Sample Feedback Questions

What do you see as the strengths of my plan?

Do you have suggestions for improvement? If so, what?

Are there ways I haven't considered that I should use to communicate more effectively with students, parents, and families about my plan?

Are you willing to provide your support (remember, be specific about what you need)?

Tool 217
Collaborating with Instructional Specialists

Many schools now have someone, typically a former teacher, who serves as a resource. This person may be school-based, or part of a district-based team. Whether called an instructional specialist, content area facilitator, curriculum specialist, or a number of other titles, their role is usually the same: to help teachers improve their practice by serving as a resource, guide, or mentor. Some also observe classes to provide feedback or an evaluation.

These specialists can be very helpful as you work to improve rigor in the classroom. There are three Bs that form a foundation for working with specialists.

> **Three Bs for Working with Instructional Specialists**
>
> Build a relationship.
> Be clear on roles.
> Begin with student learning in mind.

Build a Relationship

This may sound basic, but it's true. A good relationship is the foundation for working together. I worked with a school where the teachers resented the instructional specialist because she had been a former teacher in the school. Some of them wanted the job, and they were negative because of that. That's an unfortunate situation, but you have to move past it. An instructional specialist can be a great help to you, but you have to be willing to work with him or her. Be open to your instructional specialist, and work to be a true team.

Be Clear on Roles

Second, be clear on each other's roles. For example, in many situations, the instructional specialist is not an evaluator; they serve as a facilitator of your work and a resource. If so, be sure each of you understands the role and works within those parameters.

If the specialist also observes you as part of your formal evaluation, then you need to be aware of that and respond accordingly. One teacher I spoke with explained, "Since my curriculum facilitator evaluates me and that is part of my yearly evaluation, I'm careful that I don't ask for too much help. I don't want it to be seen as a negative." That's unfortunate, but what's important is that you know exactly what the specialist's role is and how it impacts you.

Begin with Student Learning in Mind

Finally, begin (and end) with student learning as your focus. I was in one situation where everything was personal. Feedback was interpreted as a criticism of the teacher's performance, and responses to the specialist were negative. Remember, an instructional specialist or coach is there to help you be more effective. It's about benefiting your students so they learn at higher level. Keep your focus there, and don't let it become personal.

Tool 218
Working with Your School Board

Another group you want to consider as you work to increase rigor in your classroom is your school board. They generally set policy for your school district, and it's helpful to keep them informed about what is happening in schools. Consider sharing your success with them!

> **Five Strategies for Making Effective Presentations to Your School Board**
> 1. Identify a parent or student to help deliver your message to the board.
> 2. Frame the importance of rigor in your opening statement.
> 3. Link it to board goals and how students will be successful once they leave your class.
> 4. Share examples of your work to illustrate the impact. It can be very helpful to highlight the effect of greater rigor on one or more students.
> 5. Conclude by reinforcing the benefits of rigor for your students, as well as to the district as a whole.

Working with Other Teachers

Another way to extend your reach beyond your classroom is by working with other teachers. You probably already work with teachers in a variety of ways, but we'll take a look at some of the more formal ways to work with teachers, including professional learning communities.

> Professional Learning Communities
> Personal Learning Communities
> Co-Teachers/Specialized Teachers/Teacher Assistants
> Substitute Teachers

Professional Learning Communities

A professional community of learners (PLC) reflects the commitment of teachers and administrators who continuously seek to learn and grow professionally and then act on what they learn. The goal is to improve student learning by improving effectiveness. There are several typical activities for professional learning communities.

> **Sample PLC Activities**
> Book Studies
> Common Assessments
> Looking at Student Work
> Learning Walks
> Lesson Studies
> Charrettes

Tool 219
Book Studies

One popular activity for PLCs is a book study around a particular topic. For example, you may be in a group that is studying this book. It's important to choose a book that matches a topic based on your needs.

Book Study Protocol

♦ Membership should be voluntary, but inclusive.

♦ Decide a meeting schedule, meeting place, length of book to be read, and what will happen after the book is read. It is recommended that meetings last no more than one hour and be held at a consistent time and place.

♦ Select a responsible facilitator to keep the group on task and help manage the meetings.

♦ Select a book with a clear objective in mind. For example, use *Rigor is not a Four Letter Word* with teachers to launch the conversation about rigor or use *Rigorous Schools and Classrooms: Leading the Way* with school leaders or your school improvement team.

♦ Conversation is important in a book study. Members of the group share insights, ask questions about the text, and learn from others. It is important to talk about how the ideas can be applied directly in the classroom and how to overcome any potential obstacles.

♦ Journaling is a useful way for members to think about their reading and reflect on how it might be used.

Tool 220
Frequently Asked Questions About Book Studies

How should I structure my book study? There are a variety of ways to structure a book study. Some schools have teachers work in small groups as they progress through the chapters. Other schools ask different teams, departments, or grade levels to present one chapter at a faculty meeting. If a small team is completing the study, they often have individuals share information.

How much time should I spend on each chapter? That also depends on your structure, and your school schedule. If you would like to work on a compressed schedule, you can do one chapter per week. I prefer to have more reflection time, so two weeks per chapter works as a minimum. I've also worked with schools that do one chapter a month, or one chapter a week, so it is dictated by what is practical for you.

What do we do when one person wants to dominate the conversation? This is always a challenge. While you want to encourage dialogue, you want participation to be shared. One of my best strategies is to utilize pair-share, just as I do with students. Rather than always letting one person jump in, ask teachers turn to a partner, and then rotate which pair shares out with the group. You may also choose to have a private conversation with the person, since he or she may not be aware of their negative impact on the group.

Tool 221
Common Assessments

Another activity that PLCs use is working with common assessments. This involves two separate steps:

1. Creating and/or revising common assessments to meet standards.

2. Agreeing upon acceptable standards for work.

Protocol for a Conversation About Expectations for Assessments

Gather copies of a standard assignment, such as a short essay, completed by students. Be sure to have copies from several teachers.

Share copies of the assignment with the group and ask everyone to assess it.

Meet to discuss the results. Use prompts to guide the discussion. For example, "How do you determine quality?," "What do you consider in a quality assignment?," or "What do you expect students to know in order to complete this assignment?" "How would we revise this to incorporate more rigor?"

From the conversation, develop a (or adjust an existing) rubric for evaluation. Discuss what would constitute acceptable work.

Implement the revised or a similar assignment. Meet again to follow the process above until everyone is on the same page.

Note: During the development of a rubric, it is also beneficial to discuss appropriate grading practices. What constitutes an A? A B or C? Grading can be controversial, but it is important to be on the same page with perspectives of quality work.

Tool 222
Looking at Student Work

The next step is to incorporate looking at student work. Once you have clarified common assignments or assessments, take a look at authentic student work. You can examine student work as a way to clarify your own standards for that work, to strengthen common expectations for students, or to align curriculum across teachers. A key facet of discussing samples of student work is to agree on grading practices. What constitutes an A? A B or a C? Using the process we discussed in Tool 221, take the rubric to the next step and agree on levels of assessment or grades.

As a consideration for this tool and the prior one on common assessments, it's important that teachers are comfortable sharing their work and revealing samples of their students' work. Be careful to focus on the work itself and student learning, rather than discussing personal opinions about the quality of a teacher. If you want to look at samples of student work, the Annenberg Institute for School Reform suggests several preliminary steps.

Looking at Student Work Protocol

♦ Talk together about the process and how to ensure it is not evaluative.

♦ Identify ways to gather relevant contextual information (e.g., copy of assignment, scoring guide or rubric).

♦ Select guidelines for the conversation that promote discussion and interaction. See www.lasw.org for several different ideas.

♦ Agree on how to select work samples.

♦ Establish a system for providing and receiving feedback that is constructive.

♦ Bring multiple copies of the samples to a meeting. Be sure to take off any names.

♦ Look at the work. Discuss what you see, such as "How does the sample compare to the rubric?" "Is this considered acceptable work?"

♦ Discuss needed revisions for quality work. Implement a similar assignment and repeat the process.

Cleveland County Schools in North Carolina followed a similar process to develop a booklet of standard assignments and samples of quality student work for teachers. Representatives from various grade levels met together and developed common assessments matched to the standards, then agreed upon work samples at four levels: far below grade level, below grade level, at grade level, and above grade level. The booklet provided guidance for teachers as to what constituted acceptable work.

Tool 223
Learning Walks

A learning walk is a form of instructional walkthrough, but it is organized and led by teachers. Learning walks are not evaluative or designed for individual feedback.

Instead, they help participants learn about instruction and identify areas of strength as well as need. Learning walks provide a "snapshot" of the instructional program at your school. Since you are in classrooms for only a short time you should not draw conclusions about individual teachers or classes.

Learning Walks

♦ Discuss the purpose of the learning walk.

♦ Decide who will be involved. You might choose to begin with volunteers or start with your Professional Learning Community.

♦ Determine the process including length of classroom visits as well as what will occur during the visits.

♦ Be sure everyone knows when the learning walks will occur.

♦ Conduct the learning walk and spend no more than five minutes in each classroom. Depending on the lesson, talk with the teacher and students, look at student work, and examine the organization of the classroom.

♦ Immediately after the walk, meet and talk about the information gathered.

♦ Develop a plan for sharing the information if appropriate and for using it to guide your improvement.

Note: Additional information about conducting a learning walk is available at www.swsc. org/16331022110596170/lib/16331022110596170/_files/Learning_Walk_Pro tocol_2.pdf.

Tool 224
Lesson Studies

Originally used by Japanese teachers, a lesson study emphasizes working in small groups to plan, teach, observe, and critique a lesson. Lesson studies involve groups of teachers in a collaborative process designed to systematically examine their practice with the goal of becoming more effective.

Lesson Study Protocol

♦ Participants should be volunteers but the invitation to participate should be inclusive.

♦ While working on a study lesson, teachers work together to develop a detailed plan for the lesson.

♦ One member of the group teaches the lesson in a real classroom while other members of the group observe the lesson.

♦ The group comes together to discuss their observations about the lesson and student learning.

- ◆ The group works together to revise the lesson.
- ◆ Another teacher teaches the revised lesson while group members observe.
- ◆ The group reconvenes to discuss the observed lesson.
- ◆ The revision process may continue as long as the group believes it is necessary.
- ◆ Teachers talk about what the study lesson taught them and how they can apply the learning to their own classroom. They may prepare a report to be shared with others.

Note: Additional information about conducting a lesson study is available from Teachers College at Columbia University (www.tc.columbia.edu/lessonstudy/lesson study.html). The site includes a template for conducting a lesson study and for lesson design (www.tc.columbia.edu/lessonstudy/doc/Lesson_Planning_Tool.pdf).

Tool 225
Charettes

A "charrette" is a set of agreed upon guidelines for talking with colleagues about an issue. It's particularly helpful when you are dealing with a challenging topic. The conversation tends to be more trusting and more substantive because everyone knows the guidelines in advance. Charrettes are often used to improve the work while the work is in progress and should not be used as an evaluative tool.

Charrette Protocol

- ◆ A group or an individual from the group requests a charrette when they want others to help them resolve an issue. Often they are at a "sticking point" and the conversation will help them move forward.
- ◆ Another small group is invited to look at the work and a facilitator is used to moderate the discussion.
- ◆ The requesting group or individual presents its work and states what they need or want from the discussion. The conversation is focused by this presentation.
- ◆ The invited group discusses the issue and the requesting group listens and takes notes. The emphasis is on improving the work, which now belongs to the entire group. "We're in this together" characterizes the discussion.
- ◆ Once the requesting group gets what it needs, it stops the process, summarizes what was learned, thanks participants, and returns to their work.

Source: Adapted from "Charrette Protocol," written by Kathy Juarez and available on the *Turning Points* website (www.turningpts.org/pdf/CharretteProtocol.pdf)

What does this look like in action? Let's examine a broad example of a charrette discussion.

Example of Charrette Discussion

♦ After the group has formed these questions might be used to guide the discussion. Charrettes work best with a facilitator to guide the discussion and monitor the work of the group.

♦ **Person/Group Presents Issue:** *We have many ideas about how to provide students with additional support both during the school day and beyond. One of the things we haven't resolved is how to assure that teachers will use the strategies and participate in our lunchtime and after school activities.*

♦ **Discussion:** *Thank you. What questions of clarification does the group have for the task force? Discuss the issue and let's generate several ideas that the task force can use as they continue to work on their recommendations.*

♦ **Conclusion:** A member of the task force might say, "*Thank you for your suggestions. They helped us clarify the issues and think about the advantages and disadvantages of our plan. We'll continue to work on the issue and share our recommendations with the faculty.*"

Personal Learning Networks

Teachers have always had personal learning networks (PLN), though they did not always have an official term for the concept. A PLN is a network of teachers, leaders, and other educators who are resources for your own personal learning. With today's technology, PLNs have broadened beyond your immediate circle of teachers to include educators from across the world.

Tool 226
Personal Learning Network Resources

There are many tools that can help you connect with other educators around topics, subject areas, grade levels, or other areas of interest.

Resources for Personal Learning Networks

Conferences—whether on-site or in a virtual environment, conferences allow you to hear top speakers around certain topics. Many conferences now provide handouts, presentation materials, and videos online.

Webinars—typically shorter (1–2 hours) presentations by educational speakers. Often, these are free for teachers, and they can provide a way to hear a well-known speaker without any expense.

Twitter—similar to a large teacher's lounge, Twitter allows you to focus on specific conversations (such as blended learning), but also to "hear" fragments of other

> discussions (such as a tweet on the benefits of using tablets in the classroom). Twitter is most effective when you follow hashtags and participate in group chats.
>
> Nings—online networks centered around particular topics. IN addition to discussions or forums, members can post blogs, share resources, or link to documents or presentations.
>
> Blogs—many leaders and educational specialists write blogs, or short journal entries, on a regular basis. Search blogs and follow those that you find to be excellent resources.
>
> Wikis—communities that allow for collaboration and revision of documents and projects.

Co-Teachers/Specialized Teachers/Teacher Assistants

You may have a co-teacher, such as a Teacher of Students with Special Needs, who is teaching with you in your classroom. Or the teacher of English Language Learners may support your instruction outside of class. In some grade levels in elementary schools, teachers have an assistant to help with instruction. Each of these is a unique relationship that requires special attention. The three Bs (see page 199) apply, but let's add some other specific actions you can take to make this a beneficial relationship.

Tool 227
Four Steps for Working with Co-Teachers/Specialized Teachers/Teacher Assistants

1. Be clear on each other's roles and respect each person's part in the classroom.

2. Stay on the same page. If you and the co-teacher send different messages to students, they will be confused and it will negatively impact student learning.

3. Find time, even if it's informal, to talk and plan together. Agreeing on what works and what doesn't is important.

4. Be sure each teacher is equipped with needed resources.

Substitute Teachers

Another important role to consider in your plan to increase rigor in the classroom is the substitute teacher. When a teacher is absent, too often, instruction suffers. After all, the best substitute is still not as good as the regular classroom teacher who knows his or her students. However, there are times you will not be in your classroom, perhaps due to illness, a family emergency, or a professional meeting. In those cases, there are resources you can leave for the substitute teacher that can encourage rigor, even while you are absent.

Tool 228
Basics for a Substitute Teacher

There are three ways you can help a substitute teacher continue rigorous instruction in your classroom. First, leave an encouraging note that includes your perspective on rigor. This should include a definition of rigor, some examples of rigorous instruction, and the importance of continuing to incorporate rigor in the classroom.

Next, be sure your lesson plans are thorough with specific ways you want rigor incorporated throughout your lesson. For example, rather than just saying to ask higher order questions, write out specific questions he or she should ask and include sample answers you would expect.

Finally, leave a tip sheet with ways to follow-up with students who don't answer correctly or who answer with a low-level response.

Sample Tip Sheet for Follow-Up Actions	
Student Response	**Teacher Action**
Student answers incorrectly	Ask the student probing questions (provided in the lesson plan). Have partners discuss possible answers and then go back to the student to revisit the question. Review the material, then ask the question again, but in a different way.
Student answers the question, but with a one or two word answer or a simpler response than the question requires.	Ask "Why . . .?" or "How do you know more?" Ask the student to explain his or her answer and/or to elaborate on the response.

Note: For more information, see Tool 158 in Chapter Six.

Tool 229
A One Page Guide for Substitute Teachers

Substitute Tips for Rigor

1. Rigor is an emphasis in my classroom. Rigor is increasing expectations and the level of challenge, providing support, and expecting students to show what they've learned.

2. As the teacher, I've incorporated rigor within the lesson. Some of the steps may seem complex, but that is on purpose. Please follow the plans as I've designed them so that students can continue to work at rigorous levels while I'm gone.

3. Because I've provided challenging work, students will need assistance. Please move around the classroom and provide help as needed.

4. When I've provided a reading assignment, review the assignment after an appointed amount of time. Use question stems such as how did what you read relate to real life? I've included sample questions and answers in the lesson plan.

5. If a student can't or doesn't answer the question, don't give up. Use the guiding questions provided to push them to answer.

6. If students are struggling, group the students and have them come up with three key points from the reading and have each group report their responses.

7. In a math classroom, allow the students to check their responses in a group and then discuss various solutions to the problems.

8. Before the students leave class, pass out an index card or the students may use their own paper. They will complete an exit ticket by writing one thing they learned from the day's lesson and one thing they are confused about. This is a great informal assessment for the teacher when she returns.

9. You can help hold the students accountable for their assignments. The students must turn in all completed work along with responses to three self-reflective prompts: (1) I completed all of, or the amount completed, because . . .; (2) I had trouble with the following problems, items or assignment . . . (3); When my teacher returns I will or will not feel comfortable moving ahead to new material because . . .

10. Review homework from the night before using partners at first and then have partners share answers with the whole group. Allow the students to help one another as you circulate the room and provide assistance. When they share with the group, ask them to share their partner's answer—this requires them to pay attention to and listen to their partner.

Conclusion

Extending your reach beyond your students is an integral part of your job. By reaching out and communicating with parents, administrators, and other teachers, you can truly make an even greater impact on learning.

Increasing rigor in your classroom is a challenging experience, but one that is well worth it. Consider it a journey: raising expectations through standards, questioning, and adult behaviors; increasing the depth of your assignments, giving students the support they need, providing options for assessment, and reinvigorating the environment. Extending your reach is the icing on the cake. As you travel the path of increasing rigor in your classroom, I wish you the best. You are a wonderful teacher and you make a difference, even when you don't feel like it. Be great for your students!

Reflection into Action

1. What are three main tools from this chapter you could use in your classroom?

2. Which of those three will you put into place in the next three days?

3. Are there any resources you need to make this happen?

4. Which one would you like to implement next week?

5. What other tools do you want to consider for the future?

6. Is there anything else from this chapter you want to remember after you finish the book?

References

Alleman, J., Brophy, J., Knighton, B., Ley, R., Botwinski, B. & Middlestead, S. (2010). *Homework done right: Powerful learning in real-life situations.* Thousand Oaks, CA: Corwin Press.

Anderson, L. W., Krathwohl, D. R., Airasian, P. W., Cruikshank, K. A., Mayer, R. E., Pintrich, P. R., et al. (Eds.). (2001). *A taxonomy for learning, teaching, and assessing: A revision of Bloom's taxonomy of educational objectives.* New York: Longman.

Angelo, T. A. & Cross, K. P. (1993). *Classroom assessment techniques: A handbook for college teachers, 2nd edition.* San Francisco: Jossey-Bass.

Appalachia Educational Laboratory (1997). *Questioning and understanding to improve learning and thinking (QUILT).* Retrieved July 30, 2013 from www2.ed.gov/pubs/triedandtrue/quest.html.

Ausubel, D. P., Novak, J. D., & Hanesian, H. (1978). *Educational psychology: A cognitive view, 2nd edition.* New York: Holt, Rinehart, & Winston.

Barell, J. F. (2006). *Problem-Based learning: An inquiry approach.* Thousand Oaks, CA: Corwin Press.

Beck, I. L., McKeown, M. G. & Kucan, L. (2008). *Creating robust vocabulary.* New York: Guilford Press.

Beck, I. L., McKeown, M. G. & Kucan, L. (2013). *Bringing words to life, 2nd edition.* New York: Guilford Press.

Beck, I. L., McKeown, M. G., & Omanson, R. C. (1987). The effects and uses of diverse vocabulary instructional techniques. In M.G. McKeown & M.E. Curtis (Eds.), *The nature of vocabulary acquisition* (pp. 147–163). Hillsdale, NJ: Erlbaum.

Beers, K. & Probst, R. E. (2013). *Notice and note: Strategies for close reading.* Portsmouth, NH: Heinemann.

Bergmann, J. & Sams, A. (2012). *Flip your classroom: Reach every student in every class every day.* Washington, DC: International Society for Technology in Education.

Black, P., Harrison, C., Lee, C., Marshall, B., & Wiliam D. (2004). *Working inside the black box: Assessment for learning in the classroom, 86, 9–21.*

Blackburn, B. R. (2005). *Classroom motivation from A to Z: How to engage your students in learning.* New York: Routledge.

Blackburn, B. R. (2007). *Classroom instruction from A to Z: How to promote student learning.* New York: Routledge.

Blackburn, B. R. (2008). *Literacy from A to Z: Engaging students in reading, writing, speaking, & listening.* New York: Routledge.

Blackburn, B. R. (2012a). *Rigor made easy.* New York: Routledge.

Blackburn, B. R. (2012b). R*igor is not a four-letter word, 2nd edition.* New York: Routledge.

Blackburn, B. & Witzel, B. (2013). *Rigor for students with special needs.* New York: Routledge.

Boyd-Bastone, P. (2012). *Five strategies to help beginning ELLs meet the Common Core.* Larchmont, NY: Eye on Education.

Bridgeland, J. M., Dilulio, J. J., & Morison, K. B. (2006, March). *The silent epidemic: Perspectives of high school dropouts.* Retrieved May 13, 2008 from www.gatesfoundation.org/nr/downloads/ed/TheSilentEpidemic3–06FINAL.pdf.

Burke, K. (2009). *How to assess authentic learning.* Thousand Oaks, CA: Corwin Press.

Ciardiello, A. V. (1998). "Did you ask a good question today? Alternative cognitive and metacognitive strategies." *Journal of Adolescent & Adult Literacy, 42,* 210–219.

Common Core State Standards. Downloaded November 14, 2012 from www.corestandards.org.

Costa, A. & Kallick, B. *Learning and leading with habits of mind: 16 essential characteristics for success.* Alexandria, VA: Association for Supervision and Curriculum Development.

Covey, S. R. (1989). *The seven habits of highly effective people.* New York: Simon and Schuster.

Creating S.M.A.R.T Goals. (n.d.). Retrieved August 14, 2005, from www.topachievement.com/smart.html.

Cummins, S. (2012). *Close reading of informational texts: Assessment-driven instruction in grades 3–8.* New York: Guilford Press.

DeBono, E. (1999). *Six thinking hats.* New York, NY: Little, Brown and Company.

Denton, P. (2007). *The power of our words: Teacher language that helps children learn.* Turners Falls, MA: Northeast Foundation for Children, Inc.

Dweck, C. (2006). *Mindset: The new psychology of success.* New York: Random House.

Ellis, E. S. (1991). *SLANT: A starter strategy for class participation.* Lawrence, KA: Edge Enterprises.

Eubank, T. SREB. *Instant credit recovery or instant "content" recovery for middle grades: ICR summary and implementation strategies* (unpublished whitepaper). Accessed January 3, 2011.

Fielding, L. & Roller, C. (1992, May). Making difficult books accessible and easy books acceptable. *The Reading Teacher,* 678–685.

Fisher, D. & Frey, N. (2007). *Checking for understanding.* Alexandria, VA: Association for Supervision and Curriculum Development.

Frayer, D., Frederick, W. C., & Klausmeier, H. J. (1969). *A schema for testing the level of cognitive mastery.* Madison, WI: Wisconsin Center for Education Research.

Guskey, T. R. & Bailey, J. M. (2001). *Developing grading and reporting systems for student learning.* Thousand Oaks, CA: Corwin Press.

Hattie, J. (2008). *Visible learning.* New York: Routledge.

Heick, T. (2013). *Exactly what the Common Core Standards say about technology.* Downloaded on May 23, 2013 from www.teachthought.com/technology/exactly-what-the-common-core-standards-say-about-technology/.

Hess, K., Carlock, D., Jones, B. & Walkup, J. (2009). *What exactly do "fewer, clearer, and higher standards" really look like in the classroom? Using a cognitive rigor matrix to analyze curriculum, plan lessons, and implement assessments.* Downloaded on July 30, 2013 from www.nciea.org/publication_PDFs/cognitiverigorpaper_KH12.pdf.

Himmele P. & Himmele W. (2011). *Total participation techniques: Making every student an active learner.* Alexandria, VA: Association for Supervision and Curriculum Development.

Jung, L. A. & Guskey, T. (2011). *Grading exceptional and struggling learners.* Thousand Oaks, CA: Corwin Press.

Kist, W. (2013). *New literacies and the Common Core. Educational Leadership.* Alexandria, VA: Association for Supervision and Curriculum Development 70(6). 38–43.

Lemov, D. (2010). *Teach like a champion.* San Francisco, CA: Jossey-Bass.

Marzano, R. J. (1988). *Dimensions of thinking: A framework for curriculum and instruction.* Alexandria, VA: Association for Supervision and Curriculum Development.

Marzano, R. J. (2004). *Building background knowledge for academic achievement: Research on what works in schools.* Alexandria, VA: Association for Supervision and Curriculum Development.

Marzano, R. J. (2006). *Classroom assessment and grading that work.* Alexandria, VA: Association for Supervision and Curriculum Development.

Marzano, R. J. (2007). *The art and science and teaching: A comprehensive framework for effective instruction.* Alexandria, VA: Association for Supervision and Curriculum Development.

Marzano, R. J. & Pickering, D. J. (2005). *Building academic vocabulary: Teacher's manual.* Alexandria, VA: Association for Supervision and Curriculum Development.

Marzano, R. J., Pickering, D. J., & Pollock, J. E. (2001). *Classroom instruction that works: research-based strategies for increasing student achievement.* Alexandria, VA: Association for Supervision and Curriculum Development.

McEwan-Adkings, E. K. (2010). *40 reading intervention strategies for K-6 students.* Bloomington, IN: Solution Tree.

McTighe, J. & Wiggins, G. (2013). *Essential questions: Opening doors to student understanding.* Alexandria, VA: Association for Supervision and Curriculum Development.

Moen, C. (2007). Speed booking: Creating a classroom literacy community. *Book Links* 16(5), 40–42.

Morgan, N. & Saxton, J. (2006). *Asking better questions.* Ontario, Canada: Pembroke Publishers.

Moss, C. & Brookhart, S. (2009). *Advancing formative assessment in every classroom: A guide for instructional leaders.* Alexandria, VA: Association for Supervision and Curriculum Development.

National Council of Teachers of Mathematics (2005). *Principles and standards for school mathematics.* Reston, VA: NCTM.

Norton, T. & Jackson Land, B. L. (2008). *50 literacy strategies for beginning teachers, 1–8 2nd edition.* Upper Saddle River, New Jersey: Pearson Merrill Prentice Hall.

O'Conner, K. (2002). *How to grade for learning: Linking grades to standards.* Thousand Oaks, CA: Corwin Press.

O'Connor, K. (2010). *A repair kit for grading: Fifteen fixes for broken grades.* New York: Pearson.

Paul, R. & Elder, L. (2006). *The thinker's guide to the art of Socratic questioning.* Tomales, CA: The Foundation for Critical Thinking.

Pinto, L. E., Spares, S. & Driscoll, L. (2012). *95 strategies for remodeling instruction.* Thousand Oaks, CA: Corwin Press.

Popham, W. J. (2008). *Transformative assessment.* Alexandria, VA: Association for Supervision and Curriculum Development.

Porter, C. (2004). Beyond the yellow highlighter: Teaching annotation skills to improve reading comprehension. *English Journal (93).* Urbana, IL: National Council of Teachers of English, 5. 82–89.

Reeves, A. (2011). *Where great teaching begins.* Alexandria, VA: Association for Supervision and Curriculum Development.

Reeves, D. (2010). *Elements of grading: A guide to effective practice.* Bloomington, IN: Solution Tree.

Reeves, D. B. (2003). *Making standards work: How to implement standards-based assessments in the classroom, school, and district.* Englewood, CO: Advanced Learning Press.

Ruday, S. (2012). *Recommendations for teaching common core grammar to elementary students.* Larchmont, NY: Eye on Education.

Santa, C., Havens, L., & Macumber, E. (1996). *Creating independence through student-owned strategies.* Dubuque, IA: Kendall/Hunt.

Schlechty, Ph. C. (2011). *Engaging students: The next level of working on the work.* San Francisco: John Wiley and Sons.

Silva, M., Munk, D. D., & Bursuck, W. D. (2005). Grading adaptations for students with disabilities. *Intervention in School and Clinic, 41,* Thousand Oaks, CA: Sage, 87–98.

Stobaugh, R. (2013). *Assessing critical thinking in elementary schools: Meeting the Common Core.* New York: Routledge.

Strong, R. W., Silver, H. F., & Perrini, M. J. (2001). *Teaching what matters most: Standards and strategies for raising student achievement.* Alexandria, VA: Association for Supervision and Curriculum Development.

Texas, L. & Jones, T. (2013). *Strategies for common core mathematics: Implementing the standards for mathematical practice, 6–8.* New York: Routledge.

Webb, N. L. (1997). *Criteria for alignment of expectations and assessments in mathematics and science education. Council of Chief State School Officers and National Institute for Science Education Research Monograph No. 6.* Madison: University of Wisconsin, Wisconsin Center for Education Research.

Webb, N. L. (1999). *Alignment of science and mathematics standards and assessments in four states. Council of Chief State School Officers and National Institute for Science Education Research Monograph No. 18.* Madison: University of Wisconsin, Wisconsin Center for Education Research.

Webb, N. L. (2002). *Depth-of-Knowledge levels for four content areas.* Downloaded June 28, 2013 from http://facstaff.wcer.wisc.edu/normw/state%20alignment%20page%20one.htm.

West Virginia Department of Instruction. (n.d.). *RAFT.* Retrieved on May 18, 2013 from http://wvde.state.wv.us/strategybank/RAFT.html.

Williamson, R. & Blackburn, B. (2010). *Rigorous schools and classrooms: Leading the way.* New York: Routledge.

Williamson, R. & Blackburn, B. (2011). *Rigor in your school: A toolkit for leaders.* New York: Routledge.

Witzel, B. S. (2007). Using contingent praise to engage students in inclusive classrooms. *Teachers as Leaders, 7,* 27–32.

Witzel, B. S. & Mercer, C. D. (2003). Applying rewards to teach students with disabilities: Implications for motivation. *Remedial and Special Education, 24,* Thousand Oaks, CA: Sage, 88–96.

Wormeli, R. (2006). *Fair isn't always equal: Assessing and grading in the differentiated classroom.* Portland, ME: Stenhouse Publishing.